OUR GRATEFUL DEAD

OUR GRATEFUL DEAD

Stories of Those Left Behind

VINCIANE DESPRET

TRANSLATED BY STEPHEN MUECKE

posthumanities **65**

UNIVERSITY OF MINNESOTA PRESS
Minneapolis · London

Cet ouvrage a bénéficié du soutien des Programmes d'aide à la publication de l'Institut Français.

This work received support from the Institut Français through its publication program.

Originally published in French as *Au bonheur des morts, Récits de ceux qui restent*. Copyright Éditions La Découverte, Paris, 2015, 2017.

Translation copyright 2021 by the Regents of the University of Minnesota

Published by the University of Minnesota Press
111 Third Avenue South, Suite 290
Minneapolis, MN 55401-2520
http://www.upress.umn.edu

ISBN 978-1-5179-1141-6 (pb)
ISBN 978-1-5179-1140-9 (hc)

A Cataloging-in-Publication record for this book is available from the Library of Congress.

Printed in the United States of America on acid-free paper

The University of Minnesota is an equal-opportunity educator and employer.

28 27 26 25 24 23 22 21   10 9 8 7 6 5 4 3 2 1

For Bobby
For Maman

CONTENTS

TRANSLATOR'S NOTE

The English title *Our Grateful Dead* is both playful and serious. It is playful in that it alludes, of course, to the famous rock band. And it is serious in that the words underscore the importance of exchange between the living and the dead, who are grateful to each other for what they have given, and what they continue to give, in terms of material things, social life, and deeply felt connections. The original French title, *Au bonheur des morts,* speaks of similar relationships: happiness, caring for, and good fortune, a range of positive qualities that Vinciane Despret was keen to emphasize as she develops her argument through the stories she has told from those who have been left behind.

Legend has it that Jerry Garcia and the band were looking for a new name and randomly opened a page of *Funk and Wagnalls Dictionary,* finding the following entry for "grateful dead":

> The motif of a cycle of folk tales which begin with the hero's coming upon a group of people ill-treating or refusing to bury the corpse of a man who had died without paying his debts. He gives his last penny, either to pay the man's debts or to give him decent burial. Within a few hours he meets with a travelling companion who aids him in some impossible task, gets him a fortune, or saves his life, etc. The story ends with the companion's disclosing himself as the man whose corpse the other had befriended.

The folk motif is serious and true to the themes of this work: the dead must be respected and treated properly; they have exchanges with those left behind; the dead return to help the living, just as we helped them on their way to another existence in which we continue to participate. In this folk myth both the dead man and his friend remain eternally grateful to each other.

Vinciane Despret is a philosopher and ethologist of world renown. Her work emerges from the most vital and interesting school of thought currently in the French-speaking world, one I would like to call the new French pragmatism. She has many intellectual companions and friends who may or may not agree to be identified with such a label, but many publish in the French series of books with the witty name of Les empêcheurs de penser en rond (published by Découverte in Paris), a series that will "stop readers from thinking in circles." The name is attributable to Isabelle Stengers, Despret's Belgian colleague and friend who is often cited in her work. Stengers and Despret work with philosopher Didier Debaise, and together they have taken a great interest in American pragmatism, reviving and rereading the work of Alfred North Whitehead, Thomas Dewey, and William James, names recurring in the pages to follow, alongside those of Gilles Deleuze, Bruno Latour, Tobie Nathan, Tanya Luhrmann, and, in an earlier generation, Étienne Souriau.

What does it mean to have a pragmatic line of thought, and in particular, what does a pragmatic approach to the dead mean? It means both being "radically empirical" (James) and "irreductionist" (Latour)—thought will not permit itself to stay within the circle of one discipline or one culture, allowing these perspectives to open onto ontological pluralism: sociology or psychology will never solve (and has never solved) a problem on its own, and thought that is happy to be confined to one culture is probably "turning in circles." This pragmatism is dedicated to close observation of situations from the middle (the *milieu,* as I have left it in the French) and tries to avoid larger transcendent categories, like "society," as it nonetheless welcomes ethnopsychiatry (Nathan) and anthropology, fields with much to offer cross-cultural comparisons of relationships to death.

Vinciane Despret launches the reader into a milieu of stories—a "narrative matrix" is her theoretical phrase—that build a network made of humans: family, friends, and colleagues; and nonhumans: books, archives, concepts, places. It is all about death, but death is not a concept or phenomenon *to be explained* by way of synthesis or reduction. Rather it is something that is *to be followed through* by way of stories. It is a vitalist kind of ethnographic method that effaces much of the authorial will to mastery, as she allows herself to be incited, inspired, and led (astray) by stories that always had their own coherence anyway. They have no need to call on grand narratives, theories, or philosophies, which in any case may not be sensitive to the incremental shifts in feelings that Despret traces with her subtle discourse analysis of words and gestures used when we speak of and with the dead, carried out nonetheless philosophically, with what she calls "ontological tact."

Pragmatism, then, is not realist in the sense of insisting that *of course* ghosts are not real, but it is *multirealist* in the sense that there are multiple ways in which the dead and the living continue to interact and affect each other profoundly and productively, in all cultures, which is why there are rich vocabularies, even syntaxes, striving to express these relations. This brings us to the topic of translation. The French *revenant* (meaning, notably, "coming back") has no English equivalent. I rendered it most often as "ghost," which, coming from the German (*Geist*), often translates *fantôme*. The world of spirits (*esprits*) is explored in greatest detail in chapter 7, where I translated *spiritisme* as "spiritualism," and the *dispositif spirite* uses the tricky word *dispositif.* Here I rendered it as "spiritualist movement," which is recognizable for English speakers but not quite right because a *dispositif* is also an apparatus, device, or arrangement used in critical analysis to talk of specific working formations of word and things.

I often left *translation* in place as a technical term when I could have used another word. It appears frequently in Latour's work, signaling the necessary transformative work ("the *others* through which one has to pass in order to become or remain the *same*"), not just linguistic, involved in keeping networks alive.[1] Likewise, *interpellation,* often retained here from the French, is a technical term deriving from Louis Althusser. The dead can "call upon" the living in a similar way because we are often available to (subject to) just this kind of address. I am keen on Souriau's *instauration* (recently revived by Stengers and Latour) finding more of a place in cultural analysis, where the English "creation," "installation," or "inauguration" cannot express the "coming into being of the work" that is an evolving mutual effort of the artist and the work of art. Despret elucidates it early on in the book and uses it to express how the continued existence of people postmortem is "instaured" with the help of the living. *Fabrication* is related, and has often been retained (instead of the more prosaic "build") as a technical term—it is common in the new French pragmatism—along with the more Deleuzian *fabulation* for the work of the imagination that creates worlds.[2] Finally, I sometimes translated *version* as "trope," but mostly left it as "version" because "Versions" is its own entry in Brett Buchanan's translation of Despret's abecedary, *What Would Animals Say If We Asked the Right Questions?*,[3] which, along with a special issue of *Angelaki* in 2015, launched Vinciane Despret into the anglophone world.[4]

OUR GRATEFUL DEAD

Georges

 His father was the one who drove him to the station.

 I wouldn't be at all surprised if they arrived a little early, from what I know of the family's habits. So, the father tells his son, "We are going to be a little early," and it is easy for me to imagine a little moment of shared complicity, now that they had extracted themselves from Bertha and the little ones.

 And there, still sitting at the platform, a little delayed, is the earlier train. And Joseph would have said you can take this one, that way you will get there early.

 Georges got on board. Goodbye, Dad. Take care my son, have good fun at camp. Come back in good shape. The doors closed, the train pulled out of Vilvoorde in the direction of Brussels.

 I don't know when they got the news, probably later in the day.

 There was an accident. Apparently, the train was derailed at Schaerbeek station. Georges died.

 Take the earlier train, my son.

 A few months later, the parents must have died of grief. One after the other, Joseph first, then Bertha. Both gone. They left twelve children behind: Arnold, Germaine, Cécile, Marthe, Mariette, Andrée, Gabrielle, Félix, Berthe, Suzanne, Raymond, Ghislaine. Raymond, the penultimate, was my father's father. Georges, had he lived, would have been my great-uncle.

 This is a story my father told me. Often. Very often. In fact, more often than all the other family stories, and he had plenty of them. The train still at the platform, the life that jumps the tracks, the parents dying of grief, the orphans. Take the earlier train, my son.

For some strange reason my brother and my sisters didn't know this story—and it is certain, and just as mysterious for us, that they are holding plenty of others of which I am not aware. I think my father must have had a way of dedicating stories to different people. I have acted on it. My passing it on now is evidence of a flow coming to an end, that the transmission is taking place now, but as a kind of enigma. This enigma is something I am going to try to inherit as I write this book.

1

TAKING CARE OF
THE DEAD

At the moment an individual dies, its activity is incomplete.
One could say that it will remain incomplete for as long as
individual beings survive that are capable of re-actualizing
this active absence, this seed of consciousness and of action.
The responsibility of maintaining dead individuals in being
through a perpetual νέκυια [nékuia] (the evocation rites of
the dead) depends on living individuals.

—Gilbert Simondon, *Individuation in Light of Notions of
Form and Information*

When night falls, it is fitting to sit in the dark with one's
brothers to speak of the dead. To recall those who have
passed on, and to drink something hot.

—Kristín Ómarsdóttir, *T'es pas la seule à être morte!*

A few years ago, in 2008, a book by the French actor Patrick Chesnais
appeared in the bookshops: *Where Has Ferdinand Gone?* He wrote it after
his son died in an accident, almost two years earlier. The journalist who
covered it in *Libération* makes a point of saying how it is really a dialogue:
"Yes," she commented. "I do mean dialogue because Ferdinand is there,
living, in every word."[1] For a while, the father left messages on the voice-
mail of his son's cell phone. Today, he writes letters to him: "By speaking
about you and evoking you, I am hoping you will live a few years longer,
in a different kind of way." And yet the journalist is not entirely happy
with this interpretation; she turns to the film producer, Nicole Garcia, a
friend of the actor, to conclude with her that these letters were a way for
the father to survive.

In fact, this is a quite predictable kind of transposition, one that has
Chesnais going through "the work of mourning." This is the only response
we tend to get, especially of late, when it comes to the challenge that the
defunct set up for us: "the process of grieving." Even if Garcia doesn't use

3

the phrase, we certainly get the feeling that she is drawing on the theory behind the most commonplace pop-psychological notions.[2] The fact that the journalist goes there relates, in any case, to a certain kind of move: here she is giving us a trope with which we can all agree. Not just because this trope corresponds to what has become a particular thought pattern—the idea that mourning is a sort of exercise in psychic protection of sole concern to the living—but equally because she is quietly glossing over anything in what Chesnais is saying that might give rise to disagreement, or appear very unlikely, that is: the letters are addressed to someone who is dead, and they are deliberately written in order to give him more life.

Translating the active engagement of a living person with a dead one into an autotherapeutic process, that is, into a process that rationality has no argument with, is not all that different as a mode of interpretation from the kind anthropologists have long used when they relate the beliefs and strange practices of those they are studying to a symbolic register. So, for example, when they were confronted with informants asserting that the dead speak to them, or that they have to be given food to pacify them, the researchers from distant lands, being totally convinced that the dead neither speak, nor eat anything because they are dead, concluded that these kinds of relations must occur at a metaphorical or "symbolic" level, thereby avoiding asking awkward questions of those who were engaged in these relationships. Certainly, they said, by way of translation, these people assert that the dead act in such and such a fashion, and demand offerings of one type or another, but what they really mean is that they have to be symbolically nourished, and the fact that they speak has to be understood as metaphorical.[3]

We should remind ourselves that the idea that the dead have no destiny other than nonexistence is evidence of a very local and historically very recent conception of their status. Death as something that opens only onto nothingness "is certainly the least common idea in the world."[4] This idea took root so firmly that it has become, at least in Europe, the official position. Auguste Comte's positivist philosophy that ratified the disappearance of the afterlife—in favor of the cult of memory—laid the foundation for a materialist and secular version of death. The latter became embedded in Europe in the late nineteenth century "because of doctors and hygienists getting involved in political and professional struggles against positions traditionally held by the church on the subject of the sick and the dying. While it might have had a philosophical basis that can be traced back to certain trends in classical philosophy, it was a position that at the time had the church in its sights. If death is nothingness, then it is obviously not necessary to hurry off to get the help of the church, or to any other religious medium for that matter, to open the doors of heaven for the dear departed."[5]

So, this official understanding became *the* dominant understanding, or rather one should say the "dominating" one, to the extent that it crushes all the others, leaving little in their place. What is symptomatic of this domination is that mourning has theoretically become a real prescription: "We *have to* do the *work* of mourning."[6] Because this theory is founded on the idea that the dead have no existence except in the memory of the living; the latter are bound to sever all contact with the departed. And the dead have no role to play other than being forgotten.[7]

And yet, despite the fact that this secular "disenchanted" understanding has come to the fore and fed into scholarly discourse, there remain other ways of thinking about, and being in, relationships with the dead, that continue to give rise to some, albeit very marginal, practices and experiences. Witness Chesnais, who understood the point that the dead are only really dead if we stop engaging with them, that is, looking out for them.[8] And he is certainly not alone. The people who continue, often very inventively, to create and explore their relations with their dead are numerous, very numerous in fact.

"I have a thousand reasons to be telling you this," wrote a reader of Anny Duperey's book *Le voile noir* [The black veil]. "The dead are only dead if we bury them. Otherwise they work for us; they finish what they were made for, in a different way. We have to accompany them, and help them accompany us, in a give-and-take that is amazing, warm, dynamic."[9]

With these few words, the writer grasps one of the major ideas typical of the relations that bind "those left behind" and "those who never quite entirely leave," that of an accomplishment that ties the dead to the living ("finish what they were made for" certainly speaks of an accomplishment).

If we don't care for them, the dead die stone dead. And if we are responsible for the way in which their existence is extended, that does not in any way mean that we totally determine their existence. The requirement to give them "more" life falls on us. This "more" can certainly be understood in the sense of a biographical extension, a prolongation of presence, but more pointedly in the sense of an *other* existence. In other words, this "more existence" promotes the defunct's existence, not that of the living being it once was, which has different qualities, nor the existence of a silent, passive totally absent, dead person that the defunct could become without care and attention. It becomes other, that is, on another plane. This is what Chesna is clearly telling us when he says that, thanks to his letters, his son would live on "a few more years in a different way," just as Duperey's correspondent is suggesting when she expresses the fact that the dead "finish what they were made for, in a different way." Leading a being to "more existence" that allows her or him to influence the lives of the living has nothing much to do with the so-called work of mourning. The dead ask to be helped to accompany us; there are actions to be carried out, answers to be given to what they are asking. The response not only accomplishes the existence of the dead but it also authorizes changes to the lives of those responding.

One could, in consequence, pick up on what the philosopher Étienne Souriau says, that the dead call for help to achieve this existential "more," transforming at this point the lives of those who have been called upon. Very often this accomplishment comes about quite concretely by way of offering them the possibility of finishing off jobs, which makes the dead both the creators and beneficiaries of this accomplishment.

The jobs the dead take on are, of course, quite diverse. If we remained in the register of everyday talk, they range from the simple fact of giving the living a feeling one is present through to more active manifestations, as when a dead person gives a sign, provides advice in a dream, makes one feel that there are things to be done, or even not done, replies to questions asked, encourages, consoles or comforts, or even invites the one left behind to embrace life again.

In order to make sense of this work through which a being is given more existence, and that leads it to "continue otherwise," that is, to be in another fashion, Bruno Latour borrows from Souriau the idea that all existence, of whatever kind, has to be *instaured*.[10] This term takes on board the idea that something has to be constructed, created, or fabricated. But unlike the terms "construct," "create," or "fabricate," which we are familiar with, the term *instaure* requires us to not be in too much of a hurry to embrace the idea that what is fabricated will be totally determined by the person assuming to *make* or create a being or a thing. The term instauration indicates, or rather insists on, the fact that bringing a being into existence engages the responsibility of the one doing the instauring, to *welcoming* a request. But it stresses above all that the act of instauring a being (contrary to what might be implied by the act of creation) does not come down to "drawing it out from nothingness."[11] We help the dead to be or become what they are; we don't invent them. Whether it is a soul, a work of art, a fictional character, a physical object or death, because they are all the end result of an instauration, each of these beings is going to be led toward a new way of being by those who take on the responsibility through a series of trials that will transform them.

So, when one is instauring one is taking part in a transformation that leads to a *certain existence,* that is to say, as we mentioned, *more existence,* an existence that could demonstrate, in the case of an accomplishment that turns out really well, what Souriau calls his "burst of reality." As it happens, we can speak of "reality" when it comes to the existence of the dead, as long as we are in agreement about the particular plane of reality that can be attributed to them. But things often get complicated when we ask what we mean by this term. Do we mean that certain dead people have a full and complete existence when we say they "really" exist? That, for example, they are not a product of the imagination of the living, even though the imagination of the living can be sparked? Of course, their reality is not the same as that of mountains, sheep, or black holes. Nor is it the same as fictional characters, who have their own "burst of reality"; novelists will agree that they are definitely guided by their characters. And we know for a fact that our own lives can be intensified by encountering one of them. We effectively know about their presence because of their potential to act, or rather, to give rise to action, through their capacity to affect us from the "outside." In order to speak of the reality of the dead, therefore, we have to position them according to their "modes of existence" as Latour says, still following Souriau.

Latour picks up Souriau's seemingly simple question: In how many ways can we say a being exists? Should we say a rock "exists" in the same way as a soul, a work of art, a scientific fact, or a dead person? They all exist, Latour tells us, but none is defined according to the same "manner of being." Finding out all these ways that each of these beings can be said to exist means adjudicating, for each of them, on its particular mode of existence, on the manner by which it can be said to be "real." Questioning the mode of existence of a being means situating it in the truth register appropriate to it (no one takes Cervantes to task for lying about the adventures of Don Quixote), but it also means inscribing it in the creative relationship that was presiding over its instauration. This is the problem Souriau put to the field of aesthetics: who is the author of the work? The artist, he says, is never the sole creator; he is "the instaurator of a work that comes to him but that, without him, would never proceed toward existence."[12] The mode of existence of the "work to be done" does not allow one to choose between those, artists or works, who might lay claim to the genuine origin: sculptor or sculpture, poet or poem, painter or painting? The work seeking existence calls on the painter, poet, or sculptor, and these have to devote themselves to bringing the work to its full completion, so it can be accomplished as a work. In other words, the painting, sculpture, or poem to be made claims an existence, while the artist, and this is what defines her role and her obligations, bows to this demand. She will explore on this basis of this demand and reply, or more exactly, make herself capable of replying to what it is asking for. This is what "instauring" a work means, leading it as "work to be made" to its existence as a finished work.

Starting this work of definition—describing the way in which the dead interfere in the lives of the living—for the mode of existence that allows us to come to terms with what they do and what they make happen [*font faire*], I will avoid falling into the trap by which our tradition usually captures and paralyzes the problem: it distributes the ways of being into two categories, physical existence on the one hand and psychic existence on the other. We relate either to the material world or to mere subjective emanations. This obligatory choice leaves the dead with only two, equally miserable, possible ways out, either that of nonexistence or that of phantasms, beliefs, or hallucinations. The alternative is to propose that the dead have "ways of being" that make them into actual real beings in the register that is their own, that they manifest accountable ways of being present, and of which we can feel the effects. This means taking an interest in the fact that each time there was "a being to be made," and someone alive who has received this request. Duperey's correspondent says nothing less: the dead have things to accomplish, but they themselves have to be the object of an accomplishment. This is the "give-and-take . . . amazing, warm, dynamic." Who does what, in this story, remains very fluid, as in any story where there is something to be achieved.

Of course, this takes a bit of time, sometimes even a few years, but it certainly requires the dead to be situated, in a very concrete fashion: that they be assigned a location from which "they can finish what they were made to do"; that a place has been *made* for them. Then there are more things needed: care, attention, activities, a milieu that, if not conducive or welcoming, is at least not too hostile. The deceaseds' way of being requires good manners, manners that are relevant for addressing oneself to them, composing oneself with them. It is these manners, the deceaseds' manners of being and manners of addressing oneself to them, that those left behind learn, and that this book will set out to study.

What makes a dead person able to carry on? What is a dead person holding on to? What are the right conditions to make the dead enabled? What kinds of trials strengthen them, and what kinds put them in danger? What are they in need of? What do they ask for? What do they make other beings capable of? What makes for a good milieu for them and for those who have taken on the responsibility for their accomplishment?

These questions are quite like those that ecology asks of its objects of study. This is why I can claim that my inquiry relates to ecology.[13] Because ecology studies the conditions under which those it studies exist, it stands apart from questions that mainstream science typically focuses on. When the latter asks questions to do with existence, Isabelle Stengers tells us, they most often take the form of "can it be demonstrated that this (gravitational force, atoms, molecules, neutrons, black holes . . .) 'really' exists?"[14] That is not the ecological question. The ecological question is about the needs that have to be respected in the continual creation of an association.

So, from now on the question of "milieus" is crucial as far as this inquiry is concerned. This is because the contrasts among ways of being, ways of accommodating experiences, and ways of composing with them, are going to prove to be largely determined by whether or not they are benefiting from a conducive milieu. A milieu where someone writing letters to a dead person can give rise to suspicion, contempt, or irony—or, in the "tolerant" version of this, becoming the object of consensual translations that gloss over the very meaning of these letters—can turn out to be very impoverishing, if not damaging. Theories of mourning, for example, to the extent they are based on a requirement for the severing of links, and offer relationships nothing more than a confined psychic space, can constitute a deadly milieu.

Questions to do with milieus are just as much practical ones that come up all the time, in one form or another, for those left behind. They often begin with a problem a great number of the bereaved try to answer: "where is he?" The dead has to be situated; that is, a place has to be "made" for him. The "here" is emptied out; the "there" has to be constructed. So, those who learn to maintain a relationship with their dead are taking on quite a task, which has nothing to do with the work of mourning. A place has to be found, in multiple ways, and in the broad diversity of significations that the word "place" can take on. Before being instaured, and to be able to be, the dead have to be installed.

The first question the departed ask is thus not inscribed in time but in space. It is true the question of time often comes up: "we will never see her ever again"; "he rests in eternal peace"; "she will never again be by our side"—and it seems obligatory to conjugate our verbs in the past tense. But this question arises much less often, and with much less hesitation, than the question of where the dead are.[15] In the course of our history (and as we shall see the invention of Purgatory is but an episode), we have never stopped trying to find a place to put them, to shelter them, to continue the conversation from there. Wherever the dead are active, places are designated. Death notices are exemplary in this regard. I will cite just two, gleaned from obituaries: "If looking behind you is painful, and looking ahead fills you with dread, look then beside you: I shall always be there." Or, again: "Even though I am leaving, I am not going away."

The director Hannah Hurtzig tells the story about how Benny lost his friend Matthias a few years ago. Benny and Matthias were both in an architectural collective. One of their projects led them to restore a vacation site for children, in Stolzenhagen, in the state of Brandenburg, and that is where the accident took place. They were living on-site, in dormitories. One night, after an evening that was a little too festive, Matthias fell from the upper bunk bed he was sleeping in. It was a fatal fall. A year later, Benny told Hannah just how much he was missing Matthias. When she asked him if he still had contact with him, he said he did, from time to time. Hannah asked when this happened, and how. According to Benny, it was always when he was with his children. This he interpreted as coming from the fact that in moments like that he was in a place other than his office, with less rigid time constraints and a more relaxed atmosphere. Matthias made his presence felt. But Hannah pushed a bit: where did he appear? Benny then remembered that it was always on Berlin's Kreutz-berg playing fields, where he went with his children. And here, she said, we are in agreement that it is better to know that there was a place for the meetings. Of course, we can generate a number of associations, and Benny did so: this place communicated the fact that his and Matthias's relationship was characterized by a link to childhood. They both thought of their work as a playful political performance practice, and developed the ludic dimension in each project they did. In addition, the last project they did together was designed for children. "And all sorts of stories," said Hannah, "emerged. Everything began to move, all these stories were put into movement. And we ended up thinking that all was good now. *Benny knows where he has to go if he wants to meet his friend.*"

This story gives us a feel for the way the dead can, in the way they make us ask questions, activate those who make themselves available in the encounters they provide. As Hannah says, stories begin to move. The dead turn those who remain into story makers. Everything begins to move, a sign that something there is infusing life.

A place has to be found, which also means a place has to be *made* for them. The dead oblige us to displace ourselves. This is what leads the philosopher Thibault De Meyer to come up with a completely dif-ferent idea from the generally accepted one that the dead "make space" by allowing other living beings to find their own. We have to give this idea its most active meaning, he says. The dead make space in the sense that they draw up new territories.[16] Not only do the dead give the living geographical problems—finding sites, inventing places—but they are literally geographers. They draw up other routes, other pathways, other frontiers, other spaces.[17]

Gabrielle sent me a letter in which she told me she lost her father when she was fifteen. "There was neither a cross nor prayers. Ashes. Dispersed according to some random administrative regulation. We considered ourselves strong. We were stronger than our ancestors who had, since forever, provided a place for the dead. For our part, we made death go away. Lifted the lid. We had loved him more than was possible, and now we erased him. Because this was the implacable law of time. We had to see that as normal. At the time, and not knowing why, I kept his ties when the wardrobe was emptied. All of them. One coat as well. Of course, now I know. The dead can't really die without asking us. Believing such a thing is absurd. Presumptuous. Of course, I still needed his guidance a little. Even dead. I refused to think about it. I didn't want to be weak, or mad. I wrote to him in secret. Stopping myself from looking upwards. Refused to say a word to him. It took me ages to get over it. First I had to understand that I had the right to be with him despite his death and my life as well. The first big milestone was finding a place of recollection, two years later. Yes, in the end I was like everyone else. I went to speak with the dead at the place of death. There where I would have the right to speak of life to him, and of mine. I found it. It was difficult. It had to come from a deep-rooted place in me, and I didn't go often. Finding the place. I found it. In fact I never went back. This place is a memory shared with him. And now, in the end, when I have need of him, I turn toward this memory as if to a grave that he has found."[18]

"Those who remain" thus carry out real investigations. They explore the successful setting up of relationships with care, attention, wisdom, and much interest. They create new ways of using places and have a go at composing the milieus. They learn what might be important to those who are no longer there. They ask what the dead require and how to answer them. They experiment with the metamorphoses and learn the ecology of these metamorphoses. Above all, they make an effort to rise to the difficulty of the challenge of losing someone—and learning to find him or her again.

Sometime after my father died, I asked my mother what she knew of Georges and his story. She knew less than me. But she had stayed in touch with one of my father's cousins, the son of Ghislaine, the youngest of the thirteen children.

He replied with a long letter that confirmed what we knew. Georges had certainly died in the railway accident. But he didn't know that this had taken place at Schaerbeek.

And yet, he came up with the idea that Georges's father, Joseph, was also on the train, and that he died a few days later. As for Bertha, her death came six months later. All this, he adds, is a reconstruction from what his mother, Ghislaine, remembered, and she was only four and a half when Bertha died. So, since Ghislaine was born in September 1905, he could put the date of the accident at the end of 1909 or the beginning of 1910, four years later.

A few days after getting the letter, this cousin put a call through to my mom. He'd been speaking to one of his cousins, the daughter of Cécile, another sister of his mother and Georges. She remembered her mother telling the story of how he was accompanied by a friend, Louis Pètre, who also died in the accident.

Memory is a strange thing, even collective memory. We didn't know much. We figured out a date, we assumed a place, but the friend's name remains. The story was a bit different, since Georges's father was in the accident as well. So where did this idea come from, that my father was so stuck on, according to which he advised his son to take the earlier train?

2

ALLOWING YOURSELF TO BE INSTRUCTED

When I forget them, they're frustrated at how little reality
it would be in my power to preserve, and I seem to hear
them timidly calling, their murmured reprimands to which
my distraction makes me deaf.

—Emmanuel Berl, *Présence des morts*

The anthropologist Heonik Kwon studies the relations between the living and the dead in contemporary Vietnam. He is especially interested in the inventiveness arising among those confronted by the ghosts of American soldiers, and the reconciliations these encounters allow for. In Da Nang, a guest generally receives, at the end of the conversation, a glass of water from the well. He is told it is the gift from a spirit. This first glass of water is slightly salted. The following ones, coming from the same cistern, will not be. Not everyone can taste the salt in this water. Those with a "heavy soul" are insensitive to it; in popular religious discourse, a heavy soul, unlike in institutional Buddhism, does not have a particularly negative connotation. It simply means less of a facility to communicate with other souls. But Kwon is disturbed. He admits he only tasted salt a few rare times and his hosts were incredulous. How could a student of ghosts be so incompetent in sensing the taste of spirits?[1]

If this question hits the mark, it is also the case that the experience itself makes him wonder. How can well water have the taste of diluted seawater? Why for some and not for others? Is it my body or my soul that recognizes the salt? If I cannot sense the salty water when others can, who has the problem, they or I? These questions are not looking for a solution, even though one can always give an answer. That is their performative force. Kwon takes this on board when he writes: on the question as to whether the salt is in the water or in the mouth (avoiding saying in the head), if it is normal or not to taste it, abnormal to do it or not do it, and how to understand this strange phenomenon, there is, he says, no reasonable answer. "Instead," he continues, "the experience of phantom salt led me to other events and stories, and my thirst for being able to taste like others opened a way of understanding these events and stories in a new light." An enduring historical proverb in Vietnam is, "Ancestors ate too much salt, descendants desire water." This proverb, which can be used in very different contexts, has numerous meanings. One of them relates to this story: "True human desires, in this plot, are not those of an isolated individual. It is the individual who feels the desire, whereas the origin of the desire, like the spirit's phantom salt, may be with someone else, for it is in the presence of this other that the water becomes salty. The desire to remember, likewise, can be a desire that rises somewhere between the past and the present and something that is shared between the remembering self and the remembered other."[2]

Kwon pulls off something rather rare and elegant in anthropology. He allows himself to be taught by the events his inquiry is uncovering. In the same way that the living can be called forth by the desire for memory of the dead, without looking to clarify where this desire comes from, Kwon permits himself to be necessary to the enigma of the proverb or, more precisely, he transforms the proverb into an enigma that will guide him in his understanding of the events. This is allowing oneself to be taught; allowing oneself to be mobilized by the specific type of capture the situation demands. In Kwon's case, honoring the problem means giving it free rein and letting himself be guided from that point. By transforming these questions into enigmas, Kwon resists the temptation to pigeonhole; he won't permit himself to dismember an assemblage. The act of commemoration responds to a desire where one can't decide if it emanates from the person one remembers or from the person taking charge of the memory. It is a relationship of forces that an event has got going for it; the desire to be remembered and the desire to remember "hang" together; neither is prior. Dismembering this assemblage, according ontological priority to the imaginary of the living—"this would be the *real* cause of this desire"—or to the will of the dead, would take away all its meaning, would destroy whatever it is that makes its "burst of reality," its own ontological strength, its "manner of being" as an assemblage. In Kwon's practice, an essential virtue is cultivated in these situations: ontological tact. He cares about what endows the situation with its power to exist.

In other words, Kwon is letting his research be guided by his acceptance that these questions are not asking for explanation or elucidation. They are enigmas, that is to say, the beginnings of stories that give a very specific type of work to those they are addressing: What do we do with this? What kinds of tests are we being asked to do, and what kind of animated system will make it possible for us to be captured by them?

We let ourselves be carried along, like Kwon, toward other events and other stories while fabulating that both were waiting for us, and that the enigma is both the key and the guide.

We allow ourselves to be instructed, accepting that we might meet at a connecting point, or be a conduit for two different orders of reality. In this work here, there is no will to interpret. There is just an experimentation with meanings that might become possible. I say meanings, not significations but tropes, which is to say affects that have a magnetic pull on you, forces that traverse and direct you. It is an experimentation, a putting to the test: What do I do with this? What meanings are soliciting me? What kind of becoming can I offer this? It is a matter not of explaining but of understanding in the literal sense [*com-prendre* = "to take with"]. Allowing oneself to be instructed. Making a narrative matrix out of a story. It is a machine for making stories that go step by step; a matrix of stories that are constructed out of the preceding ones, and, as they do this, the one connects with the other, not on a thread, but in the way that a web is made. This is what we might call writing in three dimensions. Any point of the frame can give birth to a new narrative direction. Every stitch that is created leads you to the next, or to another, according to the connivance of the patterns.

Stories need space. And space is created by the story's capacity to make you move, create possible meanings that lead you elsewhere, that throw you off track. Stories bring forth other stories; their bifurcations multiply: just remember Benny, Matthias, and Hannah. Space is created in the way the story makes you move, in the bifurcations it will make you adopt as it calls forth other narrations. This is the process I call the *narrative matrix.* It is particularly visible in the way Kwon lets himself be led. Another story can be added to the precedent that transforms what it signified, opening another becoming for it, engaging the narrator and her story in an unexpected way. When narrative matrices are formed, it is on the presumptions that every story will engage others (and that it is responsible for these modes of engagement) and that it engages them in the double meaning of the word. Not only does each story create new ones, and is folded into the ongoing threads that it is helping produce, but each of these recitations thus created retroactively modifies the range of those that preceded it, giving them strength, offering them new significations.

Very early on in this research, I realized that when I spoke about the possibility of this project to those around me, people were not only interested but also often had stories to tell me. These were all great stories, all different, and put together with noticeable care. They deliberately left open all possible hypotheses when it comes to attributing intentions to the deceased—that ontological tact Kwon manifests as he protects the precious enigma of the desire to remember. When I began to get a fix on the specific intelligence of events, I realized I could do no better than let myself be guided by the people I was meeting. I decided to jettison all my usual research methods. I gave up on, at least for a time, the psychological and anthropological literature (I only came back to it later); and I abandoned the bibliographical map (when a book or an article interests us, we are keen to find out what fed into it, which we then follow up, and so on, which is the usual manner of working). And I began to listen to what people were telling me, during evening gatherings, meals with friends, openings, chance encounters; not as a commentary that would be added to what I was doing, but as something that would nourish it, guide it, orient it and constitute it from beginning to end, or rather the middle, since strictly speaking there was no longer any beginning or end. In short, I wandered around looking for connections and things that matched up, with the chance offerings they provided.

People found my project interesting. Of course, I had to learn to present it, to tell its story, and I very quickly learned that the better my pitch was, the more people were interested in what interested me, and the more they had to tell me and teach me. I used to say: I am doing research on the way in which the dead come into the lives of the living, in our society, today, and how they make them act. I am working on the inventiveness of the dead and the living in their relationships, with the difficulty that the living have the tendency to be easily swayed into granting themselves all the credit for this inventiveness. Sometimes I told one or two things I had heard. I have a friend who wears her grandmother's shoes so that she can continue to roam the world. Another went off to climb one of the highest mountains with her father's ashes in order to share the most beautiful sunrises with him. Each year, on the anniversary of his wife's death, one of my family cooks her favorite dish. One of my friends used to get a regular nightly visit from her recently deceased husband. She pleaded with him to make a choice: "Listen, Hubert, you have left us, me and the girls, and that is hard enough as it is. So, make up your mind. Either you are living or dead, but don't stay like this between the two." He never came back. A young woman, pregnant, tells the story that on the day before her first ultrasound, her father appeared in a dream to tell her he was happy it was a boy. And of course, it was a boy. But the important thing is that her father made a point of the fact that he was sharing this joy with her. In my own case, I always carry one of my father's handkerchiefs. Should I be sad, he is the one to console me.

I wasn't asking for anything, but the stories came quickly. Often happily. Also, quite often, all eyes would moisten on the brink of happy laughter— it is rarely said how happy some of the dead can make us.[3] Because there was a kind of quiet magical complicity that we felt was protected by those we called upon. It was not of the order of secrecy nor of compassion; it was more of a shared interest, both intellectual and sensitive. My world filled up with stories and dead people I didn't know.

What was also notable was that everyone had at least one piece of advice to share. You should read . . . you should see . . . you should go . . . Never before in my previous research did I get so many pieces of advice, and relevant too. I had stumbled upon a very intelligent place. So I decided to submit myself to one constraint. In September 2007, I took the decision that every day for a year I would do exactly what all these people were telling me to do, without their knowing. I imposed an obedience constraint on myself, Sophie Calle style.[4] The only limiting condition I allowed myself was that of not following advice when I knew the people hadn't understood what I was looking for.

I decided to follow *all* the pieces of advice, and I entered them all into my appointment book, day after day. What's better than writing in a diary, which both memorializes events and sets jobs to be done?

I followed the instructions without questioning what was motivating the random person telling me to watch this American TV series, or that film, or to read that novel. I quickly learned that if they felt no need to justify their suggestions, it was because they were sure I would understand, that no explanation was necessary. My world filled up with mentors with enigmatic research ideas.

In a way, each of them created for themselves an image or an idea of what my research should be, and it was from this constellation of images and ideas that my project took shape. It would not faithfully resemble any of these individual desires, nor would it resemble what I myself would have liked had I taken back what we believe control to be.

This certainty that "I would understand," and that I strove to accept, had unforeseen consequences. It took my experimentation down an unexpected path. Because, truth be told, I didn't always understand, in fact not very often. With each bit of advice, book, series, film, the link did not always appear; it remained obscure. I had to look for it. I ended up thinking I had to wait.

I had to learn to trust. The trajectory mapped out by obedience to people became a trajectory of obedience to links and to works. The works themselves had to produce these links, and I had to let them work on me, without intervening too much. I had to let them connect to each other, being confident in their power of articulation and friction. I had to let myself be worked on and taught. I became an object of experimentation, letting myself be available for what the works were creating among themselves in terms of links, questions, complicities, new beings and answers that I had to learn to gather up. Finally I had found a way to break away from explanations.

I read novels I would never have read. I watched TV series that would have remained unknown to me, saw movies that would never have attracted my attention, took steps I would have thought pointless. The saying "Come what may" could not have expressed better the confidence I gained as I proceeded along this path. And in the course of this adventure, I discovered that my acts preceded my intentions, that my intentions were the product of my acts. Each event gathered its own intentional power in which I felt caught up, bait for the intentions I was making my own. No doubt this is more often the case than one imagines it to be. It is a strange reversal of will, not letting go of something. In fact, letting something get a hold. It's a different thing altogether.

But what I also discovered was that my own procedure echoed what I was interrogating, without any premeditation on my part. Letting myself be taught, "going along with it," agreeing to delegate my actions to others, acknowledging that I don't understand and making myself available for something to come along without my knowing, that the links weave themselves without my being too actively involved (which would be bound to hinder these linkages), sensitizing myself to an "it thinks" going through me. It was, in a way, allowing myself to be traversed by "ways of being" that the dead and the living explore together. And no doubt I was also learning to cultivate orders of vitality that make this availability possible—things like a lowered intensity; a retraction of the will—and harmonize it with that way in which people themselves make themselves capable of welcoming the presence of their deceased.

And, in the end, on the actual course of my journey, I keep a precious memento—*do you remember?*—like a talisman, a knot in a handkerchief that is not even mine: you don't know where you are going; never forget where you came from.

Researching the traces of the accident was not an easy thing to do. In those days, accidents were implausibly common. It seems, however, that the Kontich accident on the Brussels–Anvers line was the most likely candidate. It took place in May 1908, killing forty-one people. We can't manage to find the list of the victims. It is clear it is not Schaerbeek, but who knows if the place indicated was the right one?

I don't know why I'm so stubborn about this. It is not a matter of "verification" or of finding the one correct story. Not like correcting errors in red in the margins of fabulations. It is something else. I am spending endless hours searching for railway accidents on the internet, going over them endlessly, in case I have missed a detail that would put me on the right track.

I have to do it, is all. I am learning to waste my time.

I'm also looking for Louis Pètre, without success. I dream of meeting his grandnephews or nieces, and hearing their stories. Would they remember the existence of their great-uncle?

And yet, the solution was obvious. I don't know why I didn't think of it. A matter of finding the genealogical tree of my forebears, and I could at least learn the date that Georges died. That would put a limit on the possible accidents.

Why did it take all this time, when the easiest thing was to begin there?

Georges Nicolas Despret, born the 18th June 1889, in Laeken, 1020. Capital, Brussels. Belgium. Died February 15, 1904, in Schaerbeek. Capital, Brussels. Belgium, at the age of fourteen years.

February 15, 1904. This date is an open-sesame.

Railway-accident-schaerbeek-15-February-1904.

This accident certainly took place. And left visible traces. I find postcards on collectors' sites. At that time it was not unusual for people to write to each other on images of catastrophes. The front was for the address, there was room in the margins on the back for texts. On one of these, underneath the photograph where one can see a group of men facing a broken-up carriage, one can read: "Terrible railway catastrophe in the north of Brussels. Monday 15th February, 1904. Two dead, forty injured." And in the left-hand margin, in a woman's hand: "Dear Jeanne, friendly greetings and a big kiss, Aunt Gaby." There are other cards for sale. On one of them you can see the carriage completely gutted. A railway worker and a man in uniform stand by it. Up above, in the street spanning the track, two gentlemen in suits and hats are observing, looking over the low wall. Another shows the carriage from afar, debris strewn on the ground, a crowd staring into the camera lens. On the side, a note: a lady signing off as Leontine is asking her dressmaker to bring her a length of velvet and a swatch of her dress in order to match her hat. Life goes on in its strangely banal directions. The stuff of everyday life, Georges is dead, Léontine will get a hat, Gaby sends a kiss to Jeanne. Two other cards show the clearing up of the third-class carriage. One of my friends, Étienne, will give them to me.

3

THE TIES THAT KEEP THE LIVING AND THE DEAD TOGETHER

Of course, I don't believe in ghosts. But I doubt my imagination is good enough to invent them. One thing seems sure to me, you can't become a ghost just by wanting to.

—Emmanuel Berl, *Présence des morts*

A woman from the village of Mansfield in England had promised a close friend who was very sick that she would place in her coffin a packet of letters her dead son had once written to her. With all the confusion of her grief, she forgot. She was in a state about this until the village postman died, not long after. She went to see the postman's family and asked permission to deposit the letters in his coffin. She knew she could trust him to be as diligent a postman in the other world as he was in this one. This was reported in the *Morning Herald* on February 14, 1829. Farther down the page was an advertisement for a conference on the materiality of mind.[1]

I made the choice to let the two extracts sit together. The first story, of course, could have given rise to many others. Many other stories could have responded to it and shown that the most original kinds of exchange continue to unfold between the worlds of the dead and those left behind. They will come in their own time. The first story could have equally arisen in answer to questions about the power of obligation. This lady did not let up in her quest to find a solution in order to keep her promise, and what a solution! Would she have had the same degree of inventiveness, the same boldness, if the promise were linked to someone still alive? I doubt it. The power of obligation linking the living does not have, or only rarely has, this kind of strength. A father appeared in his daughter's dream to stop her selling his house. She obeyed. Had he given this advice while alive, she would no doubt have done just as she liked. The communicative power of dreams has few rivals.

The strength of obligations was one of the first motivations that launched me on this inquiry. But I don't want to go there right away. This question acknowledges how much the power of these obligations astonishes people, but it doesn't require an elucidation of this power. Those put in a position of being obliged are in that position, most of the time, without knowing exactly *what* is obliging them: "I had to do it, period." What people are trying for, when they respond to what is asked of them, is being up to the task. This experience has to be honored, not explained. I am going to try to stick to this principle myself, in the course of my journey, honoring what is important for something, and accepting that I will be put to the test by this importance. This means that I am going to devote myself, in my writing, and it is not going to be easy, given my research training and the habits I am imbued with, to resist the power of explanation.

In choosing not to separate the two extracts from the *Morning Herald,* rather than letting myself be guided by each on its own, I am putting down what follows in a manner consistent with my guiding method: I am committed to following things as they present themselves, hoping, in an experimental mode, to learn about their complicities and frictions. Apparently the two articles have nothing to do with each other, except that they appear on the same page of the paper. They have no other links, as far as we know, except simply coexisting. This coexistence characterizes the milieu in which the events took place, in 1829, a milieu inhabited by contradictory versions. It is not very different from ours. Every year many books are still published questioning the possibility of coming into contact with the world of the deceased, and an even more impressive number of articles and other works asserting (or based on the idea) that death leads to nothingness. It is not unusual to hear panel discussions on the radio or on television in the course of which there are clashes, often quite acerbic, between rationalists and people insisting that contact can be made with the deceased. One can observe, in fact, that these debates often demonstrate the same characteristic: those invited are at the extreme opposite poles between what are usually called practices of enchantment—the story about the lady and the postman would qualify as one of these—and practices of disenchantment, and the conference based on materialism is an example of that. The coexistence of the two contradictory versions is inscribed in a milieu, our milieu, under the heading of polemic.

Raising the question of milieu often brings about another. What are the conditions under which, at a given time, something that was not there begins to proliferate? The restless dead are a good case in point. The social sciences, psychology, and history have all taken up the problem. They want to explain it. But going about it in this way, these sciences, with few exceptions, make more noticeable an aspect of the polemical coexistence I was stressing. They make it all the more visible when they take part in the polemic, taking sides, implicitly or not. Whether they follow the materialist hypothesis, or give priority to psychic causes or subjectivity (or any other form of rationalization, even if the reference to subjectivity is the most frequent), their issue is one of analyzing, in terms of causes, most often in terms of beliefs, what is motivating the living when it comes to the dead. From there, they position themselves without fail on the side of what is called "disenchantment" in order to explain the position that is considered to be the "enchantment" one.

I was careful to qualify "with few exceptions," because there are philosophers, psychologists, therapists, sociologists, historians, folklorists, and anthropologists who have precisely tried to position themselves in such a way that they can follow their actors, not in order to "explain" them but to come to terms with what they are doing and what they are led to do, learning better ways of speaking about it from them and with them. These are the ones who have guided me in my inquiry. Without them I would not have had the courage, and certainly not the tools.[2]

Most research in the human sciences nevertheless has the aim of "explaining," without worrying too much about finding the "relevant," shareable, ways of speaking about it.

Sticking to the disenchantment line, they spend all their time elucidating the conditions for belief, or for its dissolution, because the latter appears in their eyes to be the principal cause of the return or the elimination of the dead. There are those who believe and those who don't, or, more exactly, the dead return on those occasions when people believe they will, and disappear when they no longer believe it. So all that remains to be done is to highlight the causes (social, cultural, or psychic) that make people set about believing, or not doing that.

Now, this is miles away from constituting a faithful description of the way in which people experience relations with their dead, with all the doubts, skepticism, hesitations that are going to be with them in order to be worthy of the experience. In other words, these people rarely put themselves in the situation of defining the experience according to a simple binary system, "the dead are really there" or "it's only a product of my imagination." Let's remember Patrick Chesnais. That is not where he locates himself when he is writing letters to his son. Likewise, the fact of dreaming that a dead person shares in the joy of the birth of a child, or asks you not to sell a house, does not fix the person narrating at one extreme or the other of this polarization.

But to the extent that these sciences have effects on the way people experience their relations, and to the extent, also, they produce kinds of knowledge about them that affect the ways in which the milieu is going to embrace them, then they are stakeholders in that milieu. They have an even greater stake when the human sciences' research into the causes that enable them to explain why the dead are appearing in great numbers, or stopping doing it, invokes a milieu. They give it a form, assign it a role, and sort out what the determining effects might be. How do they conceive it? What, according to them, determines the events? And above all, how does the fact of taking "beliefs" to be a primary cause (for which the milieu, in turn, will come to provide the conditions) inflect the way of seeing things? It is this diagnosis I would like to focus on.

To begin with I will propose taking a detour via the human sciences that I announced were exceptions to the rule. They too got interested in questions of the milieu, and out of that they forged an explicit or implicit definition. But to the extent that, on the one hand, they managed not to polarize the questions or categories on a binary basis, and where, on the other hand, the notion of belief played no part in their inquiries at all, they offer a contrast that will shed light, at least in part, on the diagnosis I want to set up.

The first and less common meaning of the term "milieu" is in reference to what Gilles Deleuze proposed in his *A to Z*. But I am going to go via Magali Molinié's reading of it, because it is through her that I was able to gauge its fruitfulness in the work that she conducted with mourners. It was applied, she says, throughout her inquiry, as a way of learning to follow the issues *via the milieu*.[3] She explains that following via the milieu means taking on board the issue of not losing sight of either the living or the dead. It means learning to follow them, or meet up with them, through what links them, through what "holds them together." Following via the milieu means attaching oneself to an assemblage; it means experimenting, with a lot of precautions, with ways of creating relationships with things that cannot expect to be intelligible except as relationships. It is, more concretely, a way of considering "the dead as engaged in a joint transformative process with the living."[4] No question is asked about whether the dead who come into someone's life, or who do something or other to one of their loved ones, or who leave messages in dreams, "really exist." And in her clinical practice, Molinié learns to recognize the uneasiness that is traversing a living person as "the sign that a dead person is claiming their transformation."[5] If they are claiming it, one has to answer them, and look for what has to be done to put them at rest.

Molinié's work is based on an intuition. In the same way that healers in certain cultures can cure by making compositions with invisible beings, she decided to test the idea of making the dead therapeutic allies in her clinical practice. This requires the correct mode of address with those she is working with, the living as much as the dead. She has to ask what mode of existence the dead have; in what sense can the dead be said to "exist"?[6] What is their proper hold in reality? What is their "way of being"? Molinié does not answer this question by way of a definition or a categorization; rather her own idea is that she follow what each is making the other do, how they transform each other together, how they affect each other. Their acts and their effects are the witnesses of their existences. She lists the gestures and experiences through which the living offer their dead an extra existence on another level—the act of instauration—the kind of welcome that is given to the dead's demands, the room to maneuver that is conceded them, the actions and the metamorphoses that the dead solicit, the responses that are offered to their requests, and even the modes by which they can express their dissatisfaction in a way that can be heard.

In the process, the researcher aligns herself with the actors' own instructions in the manner of understanding and of specifying. It is because they are "taken" in this relationship that it is meaningful, because it "holds" them and makes them "hold." It is thus in its effects that it is appropriate to address them—to that which their dead make them do, and to what they themselves make their dead do. The researcher will thus "take up" this level of relevance; she will be "held to" what "holds" them. To talk well of the dead means first of all learning to follow those speaking "from" them. In other words, starting through the milieu and following all the beings from there.

To speak *from* is not just to follow but also to allow oneself to be taught. This is not simply learning to map the networks of relations but getting in there. Learning "from" the dead is what the anthropologist Christophe Pons actually did in his research in Iceland. As he got involved in the task of striving to talk well to those who would help him in his inquiry, he discovers that the relevant mode of address is itself instructive, since it brings to light the way in which the dead play an active role in the collective of the living. "At the end of every interview," he tells us, "I got into the habit of asking my interviewee if he could indicate someone interesting to talk to. Often I didn't get any good tips, since they were so convinced that what they had to say was totally ordinary. One day I got the idea of inverting my request. Instead of asking to meet living people who could speak to me of the dead, I asked to meet living people to whom someone dead had spoken! Suddenly my address book filled up. One person knew that a certain other had been contacted by a dead person, and each new informant in turn directed me to others. This gave rise to new ramifications with other dead, weaving quite a tissue of interlocking contacts . . . for which the common thread from the start was the same dead person making contact!"[7] Once he got this movement going, Pons was able to derive meaning from his practice; he allowed himself to be summoned by those who summon; he followed the assignments by following the living in their own encounters with a dead person who trusted them, who mandated them, who upended everything, who made them get moving, search, think, and act. Pons learned to follow, to let himself be "instructed," to let himself be led all through the rhizome. Thinking through the milieu was, for him as well, following the living and the dead in what holds them together.

As Pons followed the path of the peregrinations of the dead in the life of the living that they made contact with, he was able to find the "right milieu." Certainly, Iceland could be considered a "right milieu." Witness

what he said about the feeling of the ordinariness when it came to exchanges between the deceased and those left behind. It is a milieu where
such relations are cultivated, honored, where one can, for example, tell
the difference between a good and a bad medium—knowing at the same
time that elsewhere they are people to be scorned, and this encourages
the proliferation of charlatans.[8] It is the second meaning, however, that
one can give to the term milieu: it is a place that can be favorable, good,
or the opposite, toxic. The right milieu that Icelandic cultural practices
constitute is one where people can speak about these relationships without
running the risk of irony or medical diagnoses. There are discussions, of
course. Some don't agree, saying they don't believe, or don't want to believe
in, the possibility of a gray area between the two worlds. Sometimes it
can even happen in a most surprisingly paradoxical way, as in one young
woman whose family was confronted with a particularly intrusive dead
person: "I know nothing about it, and I don't want to! I don't believe it
and I don't want to believe it! When this thing comes, you can't let it gain
the upper hand. What I do is I panic, I yell out, just to send it back where
it came from!"[9]

   An open plurality, and openly debated in culturally accepted
exchanges—sometimes, as we just saw, right in the middle of the same
discourse—is a sign that we are dealing with a "not unhealthy" milieu.[10]

The philosopher Ian Hacking has given us a powerful tool for studying
the ecology of beings or things with problematic or vulnerable existences.[11] He wasn't interested in the dead but in the history of so-called
mental illnesses, and he set about speaking of them in relation to their
"ecological niches." The problem he was faced with was the following:
if we think of the fact that these illnesses, such as hysteria, depression,
or multiple personality disorders, emerge all of a sudden having not existed before, that they proliferate like epidemics, and can then disappear,
then what kind of status can they be given as real things? For Hacking,
each of these illnesses is going to find, at one moment or another (the
moment also being one element in the niche), the set of conditions that
will allow it to break out. With this perspective, all the ingredients have
to be considered real, including the illness. What we are dealing with is a
contingent, unpredictable, milieu whose conditions are no doubt neces-

sary, but never sufficient, a milieu where one can discern certain favorable conditions, but none of which can lay claim to an exhaustive explanation of the phenomenon. So the milieu is an opener of possibilities; it is what leads to their "realization," transitory, but certainly real. And the milieu "realizes" itself as such, in the sense that William James speaks of a "real" becoming, welcoming new realities.

Let's go back to the way in which the vast majority of the human sciences imagine what can or cannot be a favorable milieu for relations between the living and the dead. So, among historians, Jean-Claude Schmitt brought into focus those moments when the dead, having been at peace and relatively quiet, begin to reinhabit the places of the living. The twelfth century is famous for this. It was the theater of a veritable demographic explosion of ghosts. The thinkers of the time were themselves categorical: nothing like this had been seen before.

In order to explain this explosion, Schmitt asserts that the multiplication of the phenomenon is linked to a context, the growth of death cults. And those were themselves offshoots of the recent invention of purgatory and of the practice of "suffrages"—prayers for the deceased[12]—that accompany it; this, then, would be the milieu that is conducive to the return of the dead.[13] What the historian Jacques Le Goff called a "revolution in the geography of the Hereafter" changed the game; the dead are given a second chance to go to paradise, on condition of being supported and helped by the living. So they are going to become demanding, just as they are going to profit from this biographical supplement to shower those who remain behind with advice and consolation.

Purgatory thus offers an unprecedented extension to the reciprocal chains of solidarity between the dead and the living. The former ask the latter to pray for them in order to shorten the purgatorial period of probation, but they also display their care for the living, bringing them support, consolation, even sometimes granting their pardon for conflicts that remained unresolved, or for acts that may have left a grudge. After some reticence, the Church will grasp the opportunity and propose a fairly profitable response mechanism in the form of masses and suffrages. And this, by the way, will later lead certain anticlerical types to suspect that *the fire of purgatory is boiling the priest's cooking pot.*[14]

Sure, but there is another way of putting it. One could insist, for example, along with the historian Pierre-Olivier Dittmar, on the fact that the Church became a machine for fabricating links between dead and living. Putting it like that no longer assumes giving priority (when determining what it is that "makes a milieu") to the practices of the living alone. One can no longer assert that the dead are created by purgatory than one can the contrary hypothesis, that purgatory would have been created in order to give asylum to these ontological refugees who were coming to wander earth and create havoc.[15] Then, to complicate the hypotheses about the economic stakes and put it in another register, one can imagine that the Church was able to become this efficient machine for making links thanks to a remarkable tool that the anthropologist Daniel Fabre suggests we call a "universal converter," masses celebrated to help the deceased. This "universal converter" that the Church invented is based on techniques of care and response to disorder. He notes that this technique was still current in the 1950s, in the area around Toulouse where he lived. He remembers a little girl who refused to eat. At the end of their tether, the parents decided to consult a soothsayer [*devin*], as they are called in that region. This soothsayer ended up finding signs of the presence of a dead person and he got busy trying to identify it. They suspected that either he had left behind a grudge, a debt, something that hadn't been done, or that something he needed had not been left in his coffin. The way to sort this out was then quite simple: when disorders or the repetition of misfortune call for particular responses, Mass solves them all at once.[16]

To pick up on the question of the demographic explosion of ghosts "via the milieu" would therefore require us to think the living create a favorable milieu that makes them available for certain forms of summoning. This is what Schmitt seems to do, especially when he defines his project thus: "So we ask ourselves how people in the past went about remembering their deceased, more often forgetting them, and how some of these dead . . . seemed to revolt against the living wanting to forget them, by bringing their memory back to life, invading their dreams, haunting their houses."[17] Living and dead seem to be "holding together" fairly well (but for the "seem to" coming along to modify their power to act), held in a mechanism of conjoined transformations, existing well and truly the ones for the others.

Yet the author opens his book with the very condition that in fact will impede this possible joining, and this from the very first sentence, where he announces the conditions for understanding all that will be said and read: "The only existence the dead have is the one the living imagine for them."[18] So all this was just a product of imagination. The problem is solved. The "only" is often the sign of this kind of operation. Too fast, the ethnopsychiatrist Tobie Nathan would say: "One only has to utter the following sentence: 'The memory of the dead arising in the course of an action or in a thought in the imagination of the survivor . . .' for thought to be interrupted. With such a statement, you think you have said it all; but in fact you have led yourself astray, you have interrupted the momentum of reflection by being captured by the temptation of resolving the problem too soon."[19]

Of course, at other times the action is distributed in a more equitable fashion. Schmitt writes, "Medieval ghosts . . . were the rare dead who, obstinately, and for a brief time after their demise, kept at bay the regular function of Christian *memoria*." But this proposition sees itself seriously compromised when the author again takes up his pen to assert that in fact these recalcitrant dead "created an obstacle to the necessary process of 'the work of mourning.' "[20] Here our ancestors are similar to us. Here they are, post-Freudian *avant la lettre,* and seven centuries early![21] Here they are forced into the work of mourning. And yet—Schmitt being a historian must be aware of this—this way of going about things is absolutely in contradiction of the historiographical project. Because the historian's task is precisely that of historicizing, showing how conceptions, relations, modes of consciousness, and modes of existence are going to be favored or nourished by certain specific contexts. The relation to the dead all of a sudden loses any historical form, because no matter what time one is in one should carry out the work of mourning even if one doesn't know what one is doing.

It seems to me this false step on the part of a seasoned historian reveals something else. Either he sees the need to jump in quickly, totally guarding himself in advance, and whatever the price, against any form of irrationality, or, the theory of mourning has taken on such a load of common sense that it can no longer appear as what it is, that is, a theory relative to a history and to a huge variety of factors: those involved in the fight against religious and popular beliefs; those involved in the secularization of medicine, psychiatry and relations to the dead.[22] Mourning has become what the anthropologist Emily Martin, in her excellent inquiry into bipolar conditions, has called a "text-atom."[23] What she is labeling here, after her ongoing experience with patients, refers to the fact that when they are in group therapy they tend to use diagnostic categories from *DSM-III* to describe what they are living with and the manner in which they are affected.[24] These are "text-atoms," text-symptoms, whose use translates the fact that they have become a kind of norm to describe the experience. A prescribed and imposed norm. From this perspective, the term grieving, because it implies a whole theory that guides and constrains the experience accompanying the fact of having lost someone, plays not only the part one can recognize as coming from psychological theories, that of disciplining differences, but also, in the case of grieving, that of disciplining irrationality.

In the conclusions to his book, Schmitt repeats his warning: "We have always returned to this point: the dead have no other existence than that which the living give them. It is individual and social imagination (dreams, stories, shared beliefs); and it is socialized speech (at the wake, during sermons) that make ghosts move and speak."[25] Few doubt that the dead cannot "hold on" all by themselves. Of course, we are responsible for their existence, and of course we also need religion, suffrages, ways of summoning them and, above all, stories and dreams, which are the primary vehicles at certain times and in certain places. Arrangements and mechanisms have to be cultivated, which could also be called technical availability operators. But as soon as one turns these mechanisms into sole causes, the word "milieu" changes its meaning. It is no longer an ecological niche, a set of felicitous conditions, but a set of determining conditions. A select few causes see themselves taking on all explanatory power, the whole power to "cause," and the rest become either effects or objects of causal action. The milieu is no longer the point of departure; the end is, what one has determined as effects, and one heads back to the causes. The milieu is not made of conditions to grasp, of demanding opportunities for new ways of acting or existing; it is pure causality. It determines everything. The operation is anything but innocent. In the end the milieu is but a way of delegating the origin of an action to nonsuspect causes: beliefs and whatever is going to encourage them.

Of course, we can think of a tit-for-tat kind of answer: if you need a milieu that is favorable for the *belief* in ghosts, you also need one that is favorable to *believe* that the dead are dead. But that answer, as we shall see, cannot produce anything of great interest. When you deconstruct, at the end there is always something at the bottom that stops the deconstruction, and this bottom, because it has escaped the activity, takes on the exceptional allure of inevitable reality. So, take the theologian Rudolf Bultmann announcing victoriously in 1953: "Now that the forces and laws of nature have been discovered, we no longer have to believe in spirits, whether good or bad. . . . It is impossible to use electric lights and the wireless . . . and to believe at the same time in spirits."[26] Anthropologists and sociologists followed, with the evangelistic optimism of those in conquered territory, with their own versions. Electricity seemed to appear at the time in a nonmetaphorical mode, as the very thing that was going to replace obscurity with light. Of course, electricity was able to get rid of some of the invisible things in the world. Only some. And it is true that in a universe that leaves little place for shadows, certain things can no longer be perceived, just as we can't hear certain sounds when there is no silence. So we should remember, if we want to continue to promote ways of thinking that don't relate to the triumphalist register of progress, that electricity has brought about profound changes to our ways of living, thinking, perception, and feeling, and it has done so especially by modifying our ways of sleeping, dreaming, sharing dreams, and interpreting them. The eight-hour night, which has become an almost obligatory norm, is an invention that has largely come at the same time as electricity. For a long time our ancestors went to bed at nightfall, getting up around midnight, at which time, in a somewhat sleepy state, they would pick up on activities they would interrupt for a second time by going back to sleep. This segmented sleep is still practiced in a large part of the world. The anthropologist Eduardo Kohn, for example, relates that the Runa in the Napo region of the equatorial Amazon get up at night, sometimes several times, and often share their dreams. From this we can see that the oneiric world spills over into the waking one, and vigilance interferes with dreams, in such a way that they interlock. The anthropologist Tanya Luhrmann suggests that this way of organizing wakefulness and sleep, dreams and perhaps their exchange, could have an influence on the manner that people experience the spiritual and what is called the supernatural. The semiconscious state in which dreams are mixed with consciousness is conducive, for those who practice or cultivate this state, to the possibility of experiencing things that are usually impossible. They can, for example, hear someone speaking to them from hundreds of kilometers away, feel that something has happened to one of their family, or even see things that are normally not seen. Luhrmann also claims that an American who might have what are considered in our cultures to be a sleep disorder (and would have learned to define it as such), and who is questioned about strange events happening at night, will be more inclined to describe things as unreal and due to a lack of sleep. "It seems likely," she concludes, "that the way our culture invites us to pay attention to that delicate space in which one hovers on the edge of sleep changes what we remember of it."[27]

Finally, I will note in passing that in parallel to the invention of electricity, we could also accuse natural gas, at least in England, of getting rid of ghosts. There, natural gas effectively replaced coal-based gas, whose very high carbon monoxide content could bring about hallucinations. And perhaps altered states of consciousness. This is what led the novelist Jeanette Winterson to come up with the hypothesis that this change is without doubt responsible for the fact that "ghosts are appearing to us much less often in the house."[28]

If the responses to the question about what is conducive to the return of the dead turn out to be so unsatisfying, it is not just because they give milieu a determinist signification, but above all because they are based on the notion of belief. At one time a handy epistemological tool, belief has become a formidable weapon for disqualification.[29] But I found that the research carried out by the anthropologist Angel Yankov provides a remarkable contrast. On the subject of the disappearance of ghosts called *Drakus,* he set out to interview certain very old people in the village of Dolene in Bulgaria.[30] His choice of informants is itself interesting. He went looking for those who know, people who still have knowledge of the prophylaxis that the presence of Drakus necessitated. These people also blamed electricity. The disappearance, they said, coincided with the erection of electric light poles. And yet they weren't talking about the light, or what the invention might have brought in the march of progress, but to the "currents" that disturbed the Drakus. I am all the more receptive to this research in that it avoids the elitist trap that the human sciences usually offer their subjects of inquiry, that of relating all relations to things and, especially if they are out of the ordinary, to individual subjectivity. But in this inquiry, the Drakus are ecologized.

Still on the topic of electricity, I note further that it was not a brake or a hindering factor for everyone, despite what the theologian said about it, and the echoes among sociologists. A significant statistical majority of the situations in which people experience a sign addressed to them by their deceased is derived from electricity: radio sets or lights that go on, alarm clocks that take their own initiative, broken objects that begin to work again. If electricity had compromised certain invisible manifestations, it was rapidly turned around to authorize others. As for the question about what electricity should be doing to people—bringing them out of the age of shadows—to that can now be added another about what these same people are going to do with electricity. They make other innovative uses of it.[31]

There will also be a leap in the number of apparitions in the nineteenth century, thanks especially to spiritualists. Here the explanations of these practices also attribute something that, seen from afar, looks almost like the *postmortem* riots at the time of the First World War. Some historians have summarized these practices by speaking of them as a "private denial of death." In his excellent history on the consequences the First World War had on our ways of thinking, Jay Winter speaks against this conception. Apart from the fact that spiritualism has nothing private about it, historians who characterize it in this way are doing nothing more than picking up on the official thesis, which says that the phenomenon is linked to the desire to speak with the dead. But they forget, pretty much on purpose, that there are many who thought that after such a bloody war, it would be the distraught dead who would have had need to communicate with the living.[32]

Another way the success of spiritualism is often explained is by reference to new techniques, and more precisely techniques of communication. In the nineteenth century, some thought it was the invention of the telegraph, others the telephone, yet others the phonograph. Because they disassociate the message or the sound from its producer, this encourages the idea that it was possible to put "two worlds" in contact and make them communicate. The milieu opens up possibilities; it doesn't determine them. It is this perspective that leads spectro-geographers Julian Holloway and James Kneale to suggest that researchers learn to recognize the potential in objects to orchestrate new ways of thinking and of understanding.[33]

I think these geographers have hit upon something essential. All the same, I will choose another term from the one they use, a more indeterminate one. Variations around "feeling" are at stake here, because these inventions not only affect ways of thinking and understanding objects; they also change sensibilities, they nourish other forms of availability, they engage with and cultivate other relations with the self and the world, ways of becoming sensitive to other things and to other experiences. Perhaps they offer a new capacity to feel presences, in places where, at other times, these capacities are weakened or undernourished. The idea of milieus is in need of an ecology of feelings. It is here, for example, that Winterson's hypothesis about the distribution of natural gas remains of interest. Of course, when she speaks about hallucinations, we are not far from beliefs. But it remains to be seen what the term covers exactly, if it is not the capacity to see what others cannot perceive. This prompts me to remember a recent survey of what is called "the man in the street," asking people if they hear voices or see things that others don't see. It reported statistically that those who have knowledge of these kinds of experiences have recognized musical, artistic, or poetic gifts.[34] No doubt it would have been wiser, and much more interesting, to think of all these experiences in terms of "modified consciousness." This much more neutral term, far from resolving the problem, opens up a lot of questions, calls for research, and does not allow one to think one has understood. That way one can inscribe these experiences in that ecology of feelings, different feelings in a milieu that nourishes these experiences and that the feelings themselves will change.

Apparitions, disappearances; the dead leave and come back. And we can see that over the past few years they are active again. In the next chapter we will observe their continued presence in American television series over the past ten or fifteen years. The human sciences have perceived this return and found it troubling. Their explanations demonstrate their surprise: mounting irrationality, crises of various sorts, even repression or denial of death at a collective level; and at the individual: loss of bearings, mental disorder, denial of grieving . . . There are always "bad" reasons found for coming to terms with the emergence of out-of-control phenomena, whether the Virgin of pilgrimages, unwitchers,[35] or the unwillingly dead, at the very point where the progress of rationality would justify itself on its own terms according to all things reasonable. It is for good reason that the churches are becoming empty, for bad reasons that the faithful, victims of a "hopeless loss of meaning," begin to wander "in the globalized market of salvation products."[36]

It is not a matter of not letting oneself think about the fact that the dead have started getting active again in recent times, nor of interrogating this topic, on the condition, however, of keeping the opposite question in mind: why had they been keeping themselves so discrete in the preceding period? Was it because the milieu was particularly unhealthy? Shouldn't the social sciences have something to say about this? Or perhaps they are about to realize that their attempts at exorcism have failed?[37]

So, it is not about refusing to diagnose what is happening to us; it is more a matter of thinking about the way the questions are formulated. Often questions predetermine answers.[38] Determining the causes of what is defined as deviant in relation to reason, an anomaly with respect to the common basis of rationality inherited from the enlightenment, a "resistance to modernity,"[39] can hope for no other consequences, other effects, than that of impoverishing that which is thus designated and explained, and contribute to the poisoning of the milieu.[40] It is what is called, very simply, with two possible spellings, a bad treatment [mal (-) traiter].[41]

One last hypothesis is often brought up. The social sciences link the active return of the dead to the fact that the border between life and death has become much fuzzier in recent years. The mechanisms for creating virtual worlds, and above all the medical technologies that artificially prolong life, creating dead people in living bodies, would induce confusion between the state of life and the state of death. But this hypothesis rests on an unquestioned conviction, that the border between what constitutes the fact of being alive and that of being dead would be a natural frontier, and the passage from the one state to the other would be an all or nothing situation. Now, as the anthropologist Maurice Bloch convincingly argued, that has never been the case, neither in our cultures nor in others. We have never stopped creating and exploring what he calls the "breaches in the opposition of being and nonbeing."[42]

On this point I recall an intriguing story Emmanuel Carrère tells in *My Life as a Russian Novel*. A Hungarian prisoner had been found, fifty years after the war, in a psychiatric hospital deep in the heart of Russia. His medical record indicated that during the first ten years he rebelled, fought, yelled abuse, and wrote on the walls. In the middle of the 1950s he changed. And it was discovered, when he was found once again, that this change coincided, with troubling precision, with something that happened to him in Hungary: the "disappeared" were declared dead. The death certificate was delivered to his family. "From where he was, he didn't know," writes Carrère, "but it all happened, strangely, as if he knew. The very next day he threw in the towel. . . . He was declared dead, and he was dead."[43]

"There are many kinds and scales of death," writes Eduardo Kohn; "there are many ways in which we cease being selves to ourselves and to each other."[44] The dead are not immunized against the deficits of existence. They are even more vulnerable to this in that the breaches in the opposition between being and nonbeing turn out to be, in the official academic culture that nurtures our knowledges and often judges our experiences and practices, quite difficult to access.

My quest is situated in these breaches. Along with those learning to take risks there. And who ask themselves, sometimes uneasily, and sometimes with the feeling of being happy just to discover a mode of address: What does this dead person want of me? What is she waiting for?[45]

February 15, 1904, was a Monday. In that year it was the eve of Mardi Gras. Georges was not going to Scout camp, as my father thought. The Scouts weren't created until 1907 in England, 1909 in France, and 1910 in Belgium. A Lenten retreat, perhaps?

I have the feeling that if I don't find him, no one else ever will. Now that my father is gone.

I keep looking. Plenty of photos. Then, one of them, which is not a postcard this time, on Wikimedia. Here we see two crushed carriages. The date indicates that the photograph was published on the 21st February. It came out of a magazine called Le patriote illustré *[The illustrated patriot].*

The university library has a complete run. I have finally found something that will tell me what happened.

On the first page, pictures of the Russo-Japanese war; Port Arthur after the surprise attack on the Russian fleet by the Japanese, the night of 8–9 February. This subject occupies a good part of the magazine, between the serials and the regular columns. Two Russian battleships suffered huge damage, and a cruiser, the Valada, was sunk. Among the Russian noncommissioned officers and soldiers there were two killed, five drowned, and eight wounded.

On page 89 I recognize the photograph that brought me here. The damage is shocking; the third-class carriage is ripped apart.

Page 91, an insert titled Our engravings: The Schaerbeek catastrophe:

"On Monday morning there was a bad railway accident at the entrance

to the Brussels North railway station, not far from the passageway where rue
Rogier crosses. A train coming from Anvers arrived at this point at about 8:30
in the morning. A coupling broke just behind the first-class carriages.

Two carriages were left behind, one second, and the other third class.

Just then an express arrived from Gand.

With a horrifying smash, the two carriages were crushed.

The two photographs we have printed here give some idea of the violence
of the shock.

Soon after, cries of pain were emanating. A few travelers who weren't
wounded got quickly out of the broken carriages. Unfortunately, a considerable
number of people were hurt; about thirty, several critically. Death also passed
this way. Two schoolboys aged about fourteen years; one the son of Mr. Georges
Despréz, an engineer from Vilvoorde, the other the son of Pètre, a provincial
counselor, were brought out as corpses.

News of the accident drew a huge crowd to the site of the disaster. Firemen
and police from Schaerbeek had to put up barricades to stem the flow of the
curious, and for a long time tram and car traffic was interrupted."

Despite the errors (Georges, of course, is not the son of Georges, and his
father was not an engineer but a solicitor), there can be no doubt, that is what
my father said, and my mother's cousin confirmed it. But Louis Pètre was there.
So, it was true.

There were only two dead in this accident. Them.

4
WATCHING OVER THE THINGS THAT MATTER

Now that he was dead,
all her husband had was her,
nothing but her in the world.

—Milan Kundera, *The Book of Laughter and Forgetting*

"When you cry for the dead, you will be there, will you not? When you hear an anonymous corpse speak, uncovered in a deserted worksite, you will come here, will you not? And you will cry at my death, you will say that I loved, that I was loved, and that in this world there are beings who are grateful to me for certain things. You will do it, won't you? . . . Even if no-one anywhere remembers me, you alone will remember that a man existed who also had his good points and who lived trying to do his best, you will remember that a unique and irreplaceable man existed. . . . You will do it, won't you?

"I think I finally understand the sense in your coming into the world. . . . You don't know it yet. But what made you into the man who cries for the dead, is a feeling of guilt about those endless forgotten dead, one after the other, in this world."[1]

The person uttering these words is addressing Shizuto, who is searching all over Japan for deceased people. The young man left his friends and family some years ago to carry out this inevitably endless mission. He wants to retain the traces of all those who have been forgotten. He battles forgetfulness. He stops in places where death has visited, talks to those living thereabouts, the family sometimes, always with the same questions: *Who loved this dead person? Whom did she love? What could someone be grateful to her for?*

Shizuto had to learn how to craft these questions. The way they were formulated, and their ritual process, had nothing to do with prayer—Shizuto doesn't pray for the dead; he cries for them. The formalization indicates a protocol, a technical device. These are the three questions that can reconstruct a life that can be counted, whatever this life has been. Because even in the case of a newborn they can be asked. One can think that however brief the existence has been, he can have loved and has been loved, and that there are people—his mother, father—who have already been appreciative of him, even if just because he was there, that he has taken the risk of existing, even if it was only for a few hours. It is in this way that Shizuto replies both to the question "what do the dead want?" and to their desire: they want to be remembered.[2]

I wrote about it in chapter 2, apropos of Heonik Kwon and the case of the salty water. The desire on the part of the dead to be remembered is something that calls upon the living to commemorate them, just as the obligation of the living to do so summons the desire of the dead. Of course, the actual forms these appeals take are diverse, as are the modalities they utilize or the technical procedures mediating this desire for memory or bringing it about. Sometimes they even seem paradoxical. Thus, with the Manuš with whom the anthropologist Patrick Williams has worked.[3] Their rule is that the name of the dead must never be uttered, along with the requirement that some of their belongings have to be destroyed, his or her tools not used anymore, even their favorite foods abstained from for a certain time . . . But this rule, seemingly about forgetting, is above all a rule of respect, the most accomplished form of respect: that the name or the things of the person who is no more should not be misused, so that there is no offence. Plus, this rule of "not speaking" or no longer "doing" is far from generating forgetfulness; it creates a hole in language, a rupture in habits, and the possibility of speaking, or acting, in the usual way is no match for the power of this evocation.

I have come across this desire for memory, in various forms, the length and breadth of the places my own inquiry has taken me. For instance, just to cite one, the *Remember* association draws up lists of the Rwanda massacre victims, with their clan, children, parents, and the circumstances of their assassination. "Let us give them a name and a face so they never perish . . . with a concern to fight against forgetting and the total annihilation of the victims," says a statement in an interview with the association founders Eugène Mutabazi, escapee of the 1994 genocide, and the rabbi David

Meyer. Not being dead for anyone, that is exactly the risk the dead take: nothingness. Many devices underpin this desire: names, tombs, objects that are kept, photos, stories, inheritances. This is why mourning theory creates such a dismal future for the dead.

As is well known, remembering is not a simple act of memory. It is a creative act involving fabulation, captioning, and especially fabrication.[4] That is, instauring. Shizuto's three questions are questions that recompose a life. In this regard, *remember* in English allows for a nice metaplasm, *re-member*, as in recompose.[5]

The dead can certainly be recomposed, reconnected, but so can stories, histories that carry them, that start with them, and allow themselves to be sent elsewhere, toward other narrations that "re-vive" and that themselves ask to be "re-vived."[6] It is in this sense that my quest proceeded, my "learning" trajectory from September 2007 to September 2008.

Someone came up with a "you should read" that in this respect left me in a quandary. It didn't give rise to anything. It was Herbert Lieberman's novel *Nécropolis* that Bertrand Nogent suggested on November 28, 2007. It took months and months for this novel to make sense to me, that is, to relate it to other instructive objects, and then open onto something else. Yes, it was a detective novel; there were deaths, and people who did things with them. But why this particular novel? Was that the right question? Should I have been thinking of something that the novel was suggesting and that I would not find in others of the same genre? And yet it was true that for my project the relevance of criminal investigations seemed undeniable; the dead are certainly there demanding justice. That, in fact, is one of their main roles in most of the television series that were also suggested to me. They come with demands. Things have to be done; the dead are endowed with an absolutely remarkable power to activate the living. So, I didn't entirely drop the question "why this particular novel?," but decided to consider it, at least provisionally, as an invitation to get interested in a genre, a crime genre. And since people had suggested I watch television series, I got busy in that direction.

It all began with a gift. On October 11, 2007, just as I was beginning my journey, my friend Jean-Marc Gay gave me the first season of the American series *Six Feet Under*.[7] It fit in the sense that the series takes place in a funeral parlor business. But it fit even better in the sense that the story line immediately gives active roles to some of the deceased. They don't stop interfering in the lives of the living, as in a corpse that suddenly sits up on the worktable to make an accusation. And there is the father, who having died in the first episode, reappears regularly to his son or his widow.

Others were suggested. A common theme runs through them, the dead refusing to go because they expect something from the living. The heroine in *Ghost Whisperer*[8] opens each episode with a reminder: the wandering spirits that speak to her to ask for her help are "those who have not crossed over because they have unfinished business with the living." Along similar lines, Allison DuBois, in the *Medium* series,[9] resolves some of the problems handed to her by communicating with the dead, as does Raines, the police officer in the eponymous serial, conversing with the victims he is in charge of, who don't know who killed them but can help collect the evidence.[10] If *Cold Case*[11] does not actively bring in dead people in the progress of the inquiry, that does not stop them appealing to us at the end of nearly each episode. They are there at the moment the detectives sort and put on the archive shelves the case file boxes that had been previously prematurely closed. The victims are there in the background, silent, smiling witnesses. They assert in some retroactive way the existence of a demand, by the very fact of giving thanks to those who were able to reply to them.

That is actually where all these intrigues spring from: the closing of the case at last brings peace to the dead, because in every case they disappear once their assassin is arrested. There is a doubled motif in each inquiry, punishing the guilty as a problem for the living, and responding to the defunct victims' need for justice as a problem for those called *malmorts*.[12] *Justice has been rendered*, a sign that something has been lost, or perhaps even stolen, and that's not the only problem for those left behind.

In all these series, the dead return either to claim that something should be done that wasn't, or because they have something more to say or to ask of the living.

Let's go back to *Nécropolis*. Why this novel? Any book dealing with criminal investigations would have fit the bill. I chose to think that there was *something other* than what is in the usual framing of crime fiction or series.

That should be the case, as it turned out to be. Other events would come together that allowed me to understand.

This novel has unique roles for those leading the inquiry, forensic pathologists in charge of reconstructing dead bodies from unidentified remains. I didn't grasp the importance of this singularity until during a conference I met some forensic anthropologists doing the same thing. They had no doubt about the meaning of their work; giving dead people their identities. They were reconstructing them in such a way that those who knew them could identify them.[13] Now, this newfound identity had the consequence of giving the deceased *the possibility of being dead for others*. What these physical anthropologists were doing was not undoing the work of death but accomplishing it by piecing together the remains to make dead bodies. So, *Nécropolis* does not just set the scene with enigmatic questions to be resolved, or with questions of justice or reparation. It tells how the living submit themselves to the obligation to do a good job of building a way for the deceased to be present again. These anthropologists or forensic pathologists transform corpses into persons.

I better understood how far-reaching this is when I followed Donna Haraway's advice and later read *Speaker for the Dead*, the second novel in Orson Scott Card's Ender cycle. In the distant future, a person who speaks for the dead is called to all four corners of the galaxy by families who have lost a loved one. His job is to recompose the life in narrative form. Is not recomposing the life of a deceased person like this the same as what the investigating doctor is doing in *Nécropolis*, albeit in a material register?

In this case, reconstructing a body and reconstructing a life go together, in multiple ways. It is a matter of rediscovering the traces of a life lived in the remains of the body. This is the basis for the reconstruction: signs of a former fracture; dental treatments; indications of a pregnancy; growth marks—all these events fashioned by way of forces that inflect or break. This is a life that has to be acknowledged via a kind of biographical archaeology. The dead person also has to be given a present and future existence, based on their life and body. As speaker for the dead, the anthropologist on an inquiry *re-presents* these dead.[14] So it is not so much (or not just) a matter of reverse engineering what death has done, but of guaranteeing the dead a thickness and a density, giving them back a body with limbs and a face. It is not so much a matter of identifying and understanding the reasons for their death (although this is important), but of recomposing it, giving an incorporeal existence back, materially; reconstructing a past history for them carnally, because that is the unavoidable condition for a story to continue: *re-member.*

This is the same as what is done discursively with funeral orations. In an article on the relations between the living and the dead, Molinié asks what it is that is fabricated in these ceremonies.[15] Her response is all the more interesting in that it avoids the fairly accepted analysis we see in functionalist theories, which generally explain rituals with the assumption that they help people carry out their mourning, or that they reinforce collective relations, etc.[16] A very asymmetrical kind of analysis, further-more, since the dead are only there as support act for the living. Molinié proposes a pragmatic hypothesis, an answer coming, once again, "through the milieu," to the extent that, to understand the tributes, what they do and what they make happen, she makes sure she follows the beings, dead and alive, in what is holding them together. The tributes work away at "keeping things going" [*faire tenir*]; they begin a process of instauration. She notes that during the ceremonies, each comes to speak of the dead person. And everyone who starts to speak tells either an anecdote, or talks of something that left its mark, or speaks of their humor, their wisdom, or their generosity, sometimes even of a flaw, but one that people now are clearly prepared to find interesting. Here people are cultivating the art of versions, that is to say, the art of the coexistence of heterogeneous stories.[17] And each of those left behind thus discovers something about the defunct that they didn't know. Death thickens with all these stories, these accounts that compose it in a new person, more complete, more important, denser, better linked up, unified in the heterogeneity of the versions of the self, more surprising: a person with a richer personality than she had during her life for each person present. The departed becomes more important, and more important for and with each of us, in the sense that she *imports more,* and in new ways. Tributes are processes of amplification of existence. The dead person acquires more reality here. He can therefore prolong the effects that he had as a live person in the lives of those who at present are going to inherit from him and make him live differently: to be multiple and with multiple effects, and therefore more present in his new mode of existence. The tribute stories intensify the presence; they are vectors of vitality. These ceremonies transform all involved and create new relations, as in new ways of *relating oneself* to others. It is a "becoming with" in the future anterior; from now on, he will have been. And thus, a real becoming for the future. We recompose the departed in order to be able, in the future and for a long time, to compose with them, at least we hope so. It is certainly an interesting way of thinking about what honoring and inheriting signify, in the same movement, giving a place, with its effects, to the past in the well-named future anterior: "Her presence in this world will have made a difference."

Recomposing can equally, and this is another dimension of memory in action, take the form of a prolongation, or rather an act of prolonging. Wearing one's grandmother's shoes so that she can continue to roam the world, doing things that the departed can no longer do, and doing it on their behalf, passing the baton, or even, as Roland Barthes relates in his *Mourning Diary*, speaking with, knowing that speaking is doing, and bringing into existence: "Continuing to 'speak' to *maman* (shared language being a kind of presence) is not affected by internal discourse (I never 'talked' to her in that way), but in my way of life: I try to continue living day by day according to her values: to recover something of the nourishment she provided by producing it myself, her household order, that alliance of ethics and aesthetics that was her incomparable fashion of living, of constructing the quotidian."[18] Amelie, one of the young mourners interviewed by Martin Julier-Costes,[19] tells him about her deceased friend: "Everything I do today, I half do for her, she is with me, I speak to her and I take her everywhere I go. . . . I don't explain it, it is. . . . She is in me and I need to have that too."

Prolonging an existence and prolonging it in a different way—isn't that what inheritance is?—takes its own particular forms, ones that inflect the course of a life, a life that starts as a mixture of the departed and the one they are leaving. Now it has to be completed. And completed on the basis of death, on the basis of what will henceforth be defined (thanks to the future anterior) as what it will not have finished. "Accomplishing mourning," writes Jean Allouch, "is realizing the life of the dead as accomplished."[20] Because all lives are accomplished, but it remains to be seen in what way they are—or rather, once this question is put to the test, in what way they will have been. Thomas Bernhard's grandfather, Allouch asserts, was a failed writer, but did he not accomplish his life "in being, in some way, his grandson's rough draft"?[21] One could think that the idea of redoing the departed's actions, writing the way he tried to, doing it instead of him, picking up on his ways of living, extending his habits, has a lot to do with repetition. That it is, as long as one presumes that, if it is indeed repetition, it is in the theatrical sense;[22] what comes *before* rehearses that which is going to follow.[23]

To think of the accomplishment in this way inverts the engine that repetition is driving. Past acts are not reproduced (unless it is in the sense of producing them afresh); it is those of the past that "repeat" what they constitute as future, as one says in the theatre about a play being rehearsed. The idea of the rough draft in any case leads Allouch to reject the idea, dear to his colleagues' hearts, according to which adoption, by the mourner, of aspects of the departed, some of their tics, their manner of writing or speaking, the fact of wearing their clothes, doing the things they can no longer do, would relate to an identificatory mechanism—"the shadow of the object falls on me."[24] This theory rests on a conception of grieving as a self–self relationship—pure interiority. It obscures the active relation that the living maintain with the departed. Pierre Bergounioux, narrator of *La Toussaint,* clears this up, according to Allouch, in a decisive manner.[25] He wants to go fishing with his father, just as his grandfather did. Then he remembers a scene, coming back from fishing, when he asked if they got any, they replied *bredouille* [empty-handed]. Child as he was, Bergounioux goes on, he searched for some "bredouille" in the baskets and found nothing. So he lived under an irreparable disillusionment: together, my grandfather and my father don't have the capacity to get what they want and what I want with them. The desire of the narrator to go fishing with his father had nothing to do with identifying with his grandfather. It was more precisely a matter of *not* doing as his father and grandfather did, becoming empty-handed. Apparently, doing "just like" is to be doing *otherwise,* but only has meaning as it is doing the same thing. Bergounioux writes that it is about "working to repair, through an opposite act, ten or twenty years hence, something that remained unfinished. . . . A very small ghost, from afar, comes back to disappear, and along with him the shadow of his grandfather and an earlier version of his father. I hold out to them, over the years, what they have lost."[26] In the same way, the novelist Jeanette Winterson narrates that her mother "hated the small and the mean, and yet that is all she had. I bought a few big houses myself along the way, simply because I was trying out something for her. In fact, my tastes are more modest—but you don't know that until you have bought and sold for the ghost of your mother."[27]

It might seem surprising that I haven't spoken more about ghosts than this, considering that my research has been more directed toward popular culture formations, and a good part of what guides the intentions of the dead is about demands. I have sometimes used the term ghost [*fantôme*], but always by aligning myself according to the author's semantic choice, and then often in a sense that the word does not usually cover. I would have had all the more reasons to be interested in ghosts if we were in a "spectral era," as suggested by a certain thread of contemporary philosophy, especially under the influence of Jacques Derrida. In recent years, in any case, a lot has been written on ghosts. Even geographers published a special issue of *Cultural Geographies* devoted to "hauntology" in 2008.

And yet, reading the contents of the articles in this journal, one realizes that these ghosts are for the most part purely allegorical. One might have expected in this domain, geography, that is so attached to the materiality of the world, a much more immanent, or at least more consistent, presence. These specters are there most often in the place of something else.[28] Their inconsistency is a translation of a symptom of the very specific treatment that our traditions reserve for things invisible. They are, as Tobie Nathan says, "refugees in a fearful interiority"[29]—in the collective unconscious, in memory . . .

These are mostly ghosts belonging to memory that is more or less collective (like those that were spoken about at the time of the Gulf War, when people were saying that war was going to get rid of American memories of the ghosts of Vietnam), symbolic cultural products. They are always signs of something else, something more important than they are. Sometimes they express the anxieties and taboos of the epoch; sometimes they are representative of a past tragedy or a repressed injustice. In short, these "ontological refugees" who cannot be fixed either with the living or the dead exhibit the forms of a proxy existence, as if they were given temporary passes.

To refer to them in order to understand what is happening to us would be to make a mistake that is like the one anthropologists often made when they relegated beings who didn't exist for them to the status of products of the imagination or of symbolic thought. The error is in not taking these beings seriously.[30] Referring the reasons or the causes of the relation between the living and the dead to the spectral era means one is not taking seriously either the dead or the living in who is supporting them in their existence, who is speaking to them, greeting them in their dreams, writing to them, in short, learning to respond to their solicitations.

It is in terms of responsibility that the geographer Emilie Cameron invites us to rethink how ghosts are the objects of recruitment. Far from being in agreement with what her colleagues Julian Holloway and James Kneale were proposing, that ghosts, because they represent a past injustice, can lead to new engagements in the present, she suggests interrogating the fact that, precisely, certain ghosts "represent" but without any other use than being "in representation." They are not there for themselves but for something else, in the place of something else that doesn't concern them. More precisely, they are often mobilized to mask or efface an ongoing injustice, where their presence permits it to be relegated to the past, and by this means, avoid problematic confrontation in the actual real. The spectral, she goes on to write, has become an omnipresent trope, a mortifying trope that comes along to efface the bodies and voices of those who continue to live and pay the consequences of past injustices.[31] Her research is attached to the Nlaka'pamux ghosts in an Indigenous community of the Stein valley in British Columbia. Cameron notes that a major part of the postcolonial "haunted" stories seem to have the common thread of not taking into account the *living* Indigenous people. In doing this they are "relegating Aboriginality to the immaterial and spectral past." And this is what it concretely produces, since the Indigenous people of the region say they have the feeling the nonnatives are looking through them, not (she quotes them) "that these people understand us fully or somehow sense the innermost workings of the Indian heart. . . . We mean simply that the majority of the non-natives view us as invisible peoples who really should not exist outside museums."[32] This metaphorical usage, she says, authorizes the dream of some postcolonial justice that will be translated through reconciliation with these ghosts, rather than dealing with real people who are still implicated in the situation today.

Another thing has kept me at a distance from this type of ghost, and it is not impossible that it is in fact related to what I was just talking about. I have rarely been directed down this track, probably because those advising me had a feeling that ghosts are not really the problem for those who have lost someone. You might object that François Ozon's film *Sous le sable* (2000) nevertheless has a mourning theme. Yes, I saw it, but nobody suggested it to me, and I think I understand why: because it disqualifies the experience. A woman falls asleep on the beach; her husband goes swimming. When she wakes up he has disappeared. Although everyone else declares him drowned, he obstinately keeps reappearing in her life, when she is alone. When she broaches the subject with her family, no one wants to hear about it. We see her descend into a nameless solitude. Commenting on the film, the Japanese director Kiyoshi Kurosawa said that its reception in Japan and France took highly contrasting directions: the Japanese saw it as actually to do with ghosts, while the French had unanimously decreed that it was all about a widow suffering from a denial of mourning and descending into madness.[33]

And that was actually Ozon's reasoning. In the "making of" documentary, he clearly lays claim to the second interpretation and declares never having wanted to leave the viewer in any real doubt on this question. So, it actually is about a ghost, in the French sense of the term, an illusion, an ectoplasm nourished by the disciplinary theory of mourning—nourishment that does not make the dead grow or put on weight, as we now know. Like a number of his associates, this ghost is enrolled in a polemic and a politics.

There is, however, an exception that deserves mention, that was on the advice given me by the visual artist Patrick Corillon. He made me go and see Joseph Mankiewicz's 1947 *The Ghost and Mrs. Muir.*[34] This ghost is quite peculiar, exhibiting none of the spectral characteristics I was noting. Furthermore, he asks for nothing, maybe just to be left alone. And that, in fact, is the reason for his first manifestations, as it is for many popular culture ghosts. For them, the problem is often one of being disturbed. As it happens, in this film, the ghost is a former naval captain, Daniel Gregg, who makes vain attempts, by frightening her, to discourage the young widow who has come to buy his house. Their relationship gets off to a rocky start, but it will quickly transform into feelings of respect and friendship. It turns out that at the moment when the young widow learns she is ruined and faces having to return to live with her in-laws, he offers to help her stay and keep the house. She will make her living by becoming a writer. She writes a novel that he dictates, relating his epic life as a long-haul sailor before his death. The ghost decides, once the book is finished and published, to let Lucy Muir continue on her own and link up with the living. As a device for this emancipation, he finds the idea to prompt her, while she is asleep, that she has dreamt the whole thing.

I understand why Patrick suggested I see this film. Take it as given that understanding is not about explaining, but fabulating around this question: what does he want of me? This film had touched him. What touches, I learned, and it is an important dimension of the ecology of feelings, demands relays, reprisals: "Pass what touches, touch others in your turn." What touches us relates to viral ecology; without hosts, what touches withers, and can no longer touch anyone. What touches needs us.

What touched him is that the film stages, in a fairly literal way, the question of inspiration in literature, which interests both of us, and runs through the history of our friendship. But it is not just a matter of inspiration or of writing in this story, nor of enigmas that weigh on the making of works of art. The ghost presents a characteristic that I find in many of those who decide not to leave, and I think that is also what touched him, and what Patrick asked me to act on. They don't just make claims or demands. The dead can be generous. And they encourage us to be.

On February 16, 1904, the day after the accident, Julien Liebert, who was at the time Minister for Railways, Posts, and Telegraphs, tabled a communication at a session of the Chamber of Representatives. The minutes of the meeting indicate that this request was followed by a remarkable degree of attention.

"Gentlemen, a grave and terrible railway accident took place yesterday at a station in the north of Brussels. It is my painful duty to bring this news myself to the Chamber and to the country. Just as it came into the station, a train coming from Anvers suffered a broken coupling between Deux-Ponts and rue Rogier. The part of the train that remained behind was crushed and telescoped by a train coming from Ostende, which was following a few minutes behind.

"The collision brought about the deaths of two poor young people, whose family I knew personally . . . I am even associated with the father of one of them through friendship! The accident caused injuries to nineteen passengers, four of whom were critically hurt. In addition, about forty passengers complained of concussions.

"A two-pronged civil and judicial inquiry has been instigated to seek the causes of the accident and identify responsibilities; it is not yet over. I do know that all explanations are in vain, they are nothing compared to the heartbreaking facts."

The minister concluded by presenting his most sincere condolences to the families involved, and expressed his deepest sympathies for all those touched in one way or another by this accident.

A speech was made by Maurice Lemonnier, a liberal member of parliament. He spoke at length. He had immediately gone to the site and begun the inquiry. Among the causes of the accident were cited the roughness of trains as they started up in stations, their excessive speed, the imperfections in the Westinghouse brakes that seized up the moment the coupling broke, the elimination of the tail-end car, decided some years ago for economic reasons, with its attendant surveillance, the lack of access railroad tracks at the Gare du Nord, and the fact that it is a dead end, the slowness of maintenance and enlargement work at the same station, as well as the conflicts over expropriations and who should approve them, the fact that the line was curved, the guard whose job it was to give the Ostend train permission to pass had not seen that the train that had just passed was not complete, the fact that surveillance of the correct passing of the train and the authorization for other trains to pass in turn was under the responsibility of an unfortunate worker paid only three francs a day, bombarded with audible signals that he has to understand and relay. Lots of facts. So many facts. A veritable canvas of facts that impact each other and extend, that lead off into the distance, spinning all over with their loops to catch misfortune.

Maurice Lemonnier is a lawyer and mining engineer. He knows what he is doing. He knows that if the accident is deemed to be the work of fate or forces majeures, which could easily be the case given the numerous causes that so unfortunately converge here, the State will clear itself of the duty to indemnify the victims. But if there is some fault or error, this cannot be the case. He doesn't want responsibility for surveillance to become the scapegoat in the affair, so he drives home his point: it is humanly impossible to carry out the surveillance work and follow instructions.

On the left-hand benches one can hear the voices rise, "Very good!"

Lots of stories have crossed paths with those of Georges and Louis.

5

EXTENDING THE WORK

The Generosity of the Dead

> What is important about a death narrative is that one's own
> passing away becomes a gift for those who follow, as well
> as an address to them. Death narratives are vocative; they
> call to one's survivors for some mode of response.
>
> —James Hatley, cited in Deborah Bird Rose, *Wild Dog
> Dreaming: Love and Extinction*

Captain Daniel Gregg was only a dream. This is what Lucy Muir will
believe, for part of her life. And what a dream it is that gets you to write
a novel! The term "gift" here takes on its full range, as both talent and
gift that come to you.

Writing, creating a work under the direction of a dead person, is
not, one expects, a trivial experience. Whether this is in a domesticated
[*désensauvagée*] form, or somewhat riskier, it is always operating with a
specific engagement. So, as an example of a form that one might call well
behaved, let us cite the last lines of Siri Hustvedt's acknowledgments in
The Sorrows of an American. "My greatest debt, however, is to my father,
Lloyd Hustvedt, who died on February 2, 2003. Near the end of his life,
I asked him if I could use the portions of the memoir he had written for
his family and friends in the novel I was beginning to write. He gave me
his permission . . . In this sense, after his death, my father became my
collaborator."[1] Writing on behalf of, or more accurately, writing "from"
someone else . . .

There are other more unusual situations, and they always have their
problems, in which writing, working, creating, are subject to a more
prescriptive enrollment. Problems for someone to whom this gift arrives,
and their life is turned upside down, and for those to whom this variant
is proposed. This is all the more crucial, for the former, in that the metamorphosis often turns out to be very demanding. Augustin Lesage was

thirty-five in 1911, in Ferfay, in the north of France. Deep in the mine where
he was a laborer, he hears a voice: "One day you will be a painter." This
seems unlikely to him; he barely finished primary school, and he had never
touched a paintbrush in his life. The voice comes back, insistent. It orders
him to buy a precise set of materials and get to work. The first painting
turns out to be a real marvel. For the rest of his life, Lesage will end up
painting nearly eight hundred canvases, some of which are celebrated as
masterpieces. Despite being the precursor, he is considered today as one
of the leaders of *art brut,* or outsider art. In the first instance, he painted
under the direction of his sister who had died at the age of three, after that
he was taken over and guided by Leonardo da Vinci. In 1924, he decided to
sign his canvases with his own name, while at the same time placing his
work under the protection of Marius de Tyane. Lesage attended spiritualist
circles, who could accommodate this abnormal experience, which was of
course the object of rationalizations, especially on the part of critics. Jean
Dubuffet, for example, was convinced that Lesage was exemplary of an
idea he ardently defended, according to which inspiration has no firm link
to culture at all. Dubuffet, in fact, never stopped criticizing the idea that
creation is inseparable from the culture from which it draws the substance
of its works, and defends the contrary view that inspiration and culture are
opposed: an authentic creation can only emerge from the inner resources
of the artist.[2] And yet this authentic creation cannot be related back to
mysterious entities. From spiritualist beliefs, Lesage forged an alibi for
himself to legitimate his creation. He was too modest, or too respectful
of mainstream ideas, to take on sole authorship of his works in the face of
the cultural authorities. Michel Thévoz later replayed Dubuffet's hypothesis, but loaded it with unconscious reasons, the only solution, according
to him, to pay tribute to Lesage's integrity. Lesage claims to deny earlier
influence and attributes his creation to spirits—this is not seen by Thévoz
as any kind of deceit or proof of naïveté, but as a "proletarian alternative
to the artistic trajectory itself." "Lesage," he continues, "unconsciously
had the stratagem to make his pictorial creation deviate through spiritual
mediums, and thus to find a breach in the sociocultural dike."[3]

Other rationalizations are, of course, still possible. Rationalization,
after all, does not commit to much. It just translates a certain type of
engagement. Often just being careful. But others can be looked for that

might give the problem the chance of communicating with other stories, and which do not assume one has to be skeptical about the reality of the beings engaged. For example, it is a little more promising when Michel Thévoz suggests that "it is significant that the authors of art brut belong to milieus that are furthest away from the culture of 'cultivated' people, and that one finds among them as many mad (or supposedly mad) people, delinquents, the poor, the old, women." In this respect, one could say, in reference to something Jean Baudrillard said, that art brut is the "folklore of excommunication." Now, among the successive divisions that have marked the development of Western culture, that of death is the most radical. As well, the dead have played an extraordinarily fruitful part in many works of art brut, through the bias of spiritualism.[4] Seeing the conditions for the fabrication of a work as evidence of an alliance among the excommunicated is not ceding to the reflex to distribute all the action between those who "really exist" and those who might just be a figment of the imagination. But it certainly obliges us to reconsider what it is in these ways of giving accounts of it, and in these inequitable distributions, that may turn out to be accomplices to these excommunications.

We can equally explore what we might learn from these experiences, or at least the pathways they open as we pay attention to the fact that the voices appeared in the mine. If we think about what Jeanette Winterson said about the influence of the emanations of gas, one could jump to the conclusion that these would be hallucinations. But such steps could be slowed down; they could be made to hesitate a bit, because hesitation means triggering several impetuses in several directions. A translation can be offered that opens things up, induces hesitation, and gives rise to others. Tanya Luhrmann's ideas can be revisited to imagine that regimes of wakefulness and sleep, night and day, are very different down the mine, something that makes us translate "hallucination" via an unusual and rarely shared mode of perception. This means thinking, after the philosopher William James, that modifications of consciousness don't provide an explanation of the problem, but that they lead to a different take on it, not in the light of pathologies, but as something that should incite us to throw into question the conception of consciousness itself. What do these modifications make consciousness capable of? What do they give access to that consciousness cannot grasp in its so-called normal state?[5] So,

modifications of consciousness do not represent a solution in the sense that
they would allow for the distribution of what might be "real" inasmuch as
it is perceived by the consciousness we normally have of things and that
would be "not real." Modifications of consciousness open consciousness
to another level of reality and we can only say that they make felt what is
going on or, more precisely, they *respond to the appeal to feel* what is going
on.[6] In this respect they constitute an enigma. Just like inspiration. And
dreams. Enigma, inspiration, dream: three key places where interpellations
are produced, interruptions, stimuli to thought.

In his autobiography, the singer and musician Dave Van Ronk, one of the
key players in what has been called the "folk revival" at the beginning of the
1960s in the United States, spends a few pages speaking of his admiration
for Gary Davis, the old blues musician. Davis was a blind clergyman, and
from him Van Ronk learned, more than from anyone, how to master the
guitar. He describes the sessions they had together where he was fascinated
by the old man's technique. He asked him to play certain pieces, or certain
riffs, so he could learn to copy them. Van Ronk constantly came up against
technical difficulties. He specifies one in particular that he never managed
to master despite repeated efforts. Gary Davis died in 1972. Sometime later
Van Ronk has a dream in the course of which he finds himself attending
a Gary Davis concert, in the front row. As he comes to play the passage
in question that his pupil found too hard, the reverend slows his pace and
leans toward the first row where Van Ronk is observing him, as if to show
him the technique, to get the hang of it one last time. Waking up the next
morning, Van Ronk picks up his guitar, tries the passage in question, and
plays it right for the first time.[7]

We can recognize in this story the hallmark of stories that the dead
convoke. They are situations that manifest the mobilizing power of the
enigmatic. It is a story that brings up any number of hypotheses, none of
which can pretend to dominate the others. It demands, like others I have
relayed, what the poet John Keats called "Negative Capability," "the fact
of making peace with ambiguity, to remain with the difficulty of contradictions and not knowing, welcoming the plurality of versions."[8] Of all
the modes utilized in the cultivating of this polyphony of variants, one

has already drawn our attention: the dead never act in a direct manner. They have special ways of being present that are rendered particularly perceptible by semantic and syntactic choices that allow us to describe the ways in which they act, and which Bruno Latour has taught us to recognize. It is a matter of *influencing, forcing, fashioning,* or even more clearly, *making one do [faire-faire]*.[9] These syntactic forms qualify what they are capable of, that is to say, their ways of being, their ethology, their singular powers. Other terms can be added, all characteristic of these particular ways of making present, whether they are in the register of summoning, authorizing, calling, making possible, inducing, inciting, enrolling, inviting, mobilizing, instructing, generating, claiming, regenerating, if not disturbing or prohibiting; or again, the particular regimes of actions that awaken certain forms of availability. All these verbs have the remarkable quality of leaving the question of the origin of the action totally open and indeterminate. "Inspiring" is still not on the list, and it is certainly a key register for these types of encounters, especially because inspiration leaves untouched the enigma of its origin. This is the mode through which we best feel that the question of mastery, and of the intentions that make us act, is much more complicated than what the usual action scenarios allow us to think. And no doubt also because in our everyday lives inspiration never blossoms so well as in dreams, these marvelous devices for luring or collecting signs, and for touching other worlds.

At the beginning of this book, when I brought up the surprising power of the obligations that the dead lay on the living, I mentioned the young woman who dreamt about her father asking her not to sell the house. "The last time that we planned to sell the house," she tells us, "I dreamt about the house. He came and he told us: 'Come on, climb up to the attic, there is going to be a storm.' We watched this storm through the window; it was bits of rocks, wind, ocean. This house saved us, with him. He is the one who said to us, 'You have to keep it,' *in a particular way*. And that, it's in our dream, I dreamt it. Yes, there are dreams like that. And then, in the end, we decided to keep the house, not to sell it."[10]

The dream speaks, as she says quite rightly, "in a particular way." That is where its language and its mode of address lie. It is to "this way" that

Samia decided to do justice. Here, in the doing of it, there is quite a task of sign reading and putting signs together—the storm, the attic, the warning, the view through the window, the realization, in the sense of translating into action the warning that was given. As with any oracular statement, one registers indicators and indications. And this dream is an example of that. It *is* an oracular proposal. It is all the more so if one takes into consideration, as does the philosopher Marcos Mateos, that "the oracle does not say what is waiting for you in the future. It formulates what is getting to you, what can get to you in some moment 'to be lived.' "[11] It doesn't announce, it asks for us to agree to pay attention, in the sense making oneself available to the event, by "being on the alert." It doesn't speak the future, it opens up "possibles" that had not been noticed.[12]

This dream is still oracular if we take into account that the dreamer is not the author of their dream, in the sense we usually speak of someone being the author of their acts.[13] She is the addressee, at best the mediator, sometimes both. That's what Samia confirms when she says, "And that, it's in *our* dream, I dreamt it." Message received; there was someone at the address indicated. Someone, the "I" who has dreamt "our dream," was there to welcome it.

And finally, this dream is oracular in that it asks the dreamer to attach herself to the conditions of utterance, to apply herself to the whole task of making connections, translations, relations. The dream asks the person addressed to learn to formulate it like a question to which it is a matter of responding actively: "What does he want of me?" One has no need to know if it is the dream doing the wanting, or the father. And this is why one so often hears, as an outcome of this kind of dream, "What do we do with that?"

Mateos suggests a way of replying to "What do we do with that?": "Well, let's make it an enigma." "But," he adds, "who still knows how to formulate such a thing? I just understood why Nietzsche said he was a friend of enigmas and no friend of wisdom. Enigmatic responses, that was what oracular signs were. They were made to be thought through, to make us gather forces in order to overcome trials."[14] The dream, therefore, is not an enigma, but it obliges us to make one up. It *constitutes* an enigma, in the strong sense of constitute.

Make them dream. This is one of the most significant modes through which the dead take care of the living, putting them to work on enigmas, making the course of their activities bifurcate, inciting them to break with habits, obliging them to grasp things differently. A dream, as is encountered in many cultures (the psychiatrist Jean-Marie Lemaire told me he had heard this related in a clinical session in Algeria; the historian Pierre-Olivier Dittmar, for his part, read it in a text from the Middle Ages), puts the dreamer and a dead family member in the presence of each other. In the first, told in Algeria, a daughter saw her mother painfully buckled under the burden of two enormous urns. In the second, there is a son who appears to his mother. He is among a group of men, walking very slowly keeping to the rear. In both, the dreamers are going to be disturbed: "What is this heavy load?" the daughter will say to her mother. "Why do you remain behind?" the mother will say to her son. The reply is the same. The mother shows the urns, the son opens his cape and shows a pocket full of water: because I have to carry these tears. They are yours. In this way the dead are able to participate, as I heard it nicely put, in these "little schemes of desire" by authorizing something that could only be accepted as coming from them: the order to begin life's journey again, sometimes the joyous path. The dead are concerned about grief. The living honor their obligations. They all—with that special kind of tact, the ontological tact that these situations call for—learn to address each other through the milieu.

One might think that there is not really any enigma. Quite the contrary. Enigmas, as they should, still come *afterward* here. Some questions, of course, are resolved in the dream itself. In the dream the dreamer has already been put to work, where he can directly quiz the person calling on him. But the enigma still remains to be fabricated, and prolonged. Witness the open possibility of different interpretations, little schemes of desire, the concern the dead have for the living . . .

My friend Serge Gutwirth reported to me a story that is very close to these accounts. His mother, who had been living for two years through a widowhood that was particularly difficult and very painful, told him that her husband, Serge's father, came to her to admonish her for not paying enough attention to their son's grief. My colleague, the sociologist Catherine Mougenot, told me that sometime after the death of her father, a death she seemed to live through without too much difficulty, she had a really bad bicycle fall that laid her up for a long time. Now, her grandfather, her father's father, was an absolutely remarkable cyclist, with a peerless dexterity that she might have inherited. Shortly after the fall, she dreamt of him. She reproached him in the dream: "Grandfather, why did you let me fall?" He replied, "I wanted you to mourn your father." She straightaway profited from the weeks of rest the fall forced on her to let the grief arrive.

The dead often take care of the living through an intermediary person. Once again, it is their ways of being that are in play, their own ethology, the singularity of what makes them capable. The enigma that they address leaves open the question of knowing: these stories are taking care of someone, but of whom? Who is the designated beneficiary? And who is the intermediary?[15] Yet I still keep close to me the undeniable fact that these questions, which cannot be resolved with answers, contribute to substantiating the idea that with these dream-enigmas of demands, mediations, reprimands, new stories sometimes open up, just where one thought their "possibles" had been extinguished. The stories of the dead are cultivated as an art of consequences.

Based on the preceding, you could say that behind what might be likened to a complaint, there is therefore something else, like the dead's attention to those to whom this complaint is destined, as a concern, an involvement. What seems to constitute an "order" is sometimes the sign of a restoration of order, an active aid against disorder that might be able to settle in.[16] According to Christophe Pons's work in Iceland, the deceased are frequently visiting oneiric spaces for all sorts of reasons. These can range from the visitant asking if an expected baby can carry their name (and in doing this sometimes announcing the happy event, or its sex) through to warnings of danger, other precautions or concerns to be raised. One of his informants told him that a woman had come into her dream once in order to tell her she wasn't happy, as she put it, with what her daughter "was up to at the moment," and that she asked her to let this be known.[17] So the dreamer set off looking for the person she was talking about. In the end she found out that the person in question was a friend living some distance away who had just lost her mother. She telephoned her: "What are you doing at the moment? I saw your mum, who told me to tell you that she isn't happy with what you are up to." The friend confessed that she was in the process of selling a dresser that her mother was wanting her not to get rid of. So the daughter went back to the dealer and succeeded in convincing him to return the item of furniture, which he did. The mother came back into a dream to thank her. Despite this dream being very precise as to why she was visiting, it remained very evasive as to who was involved, and how the message should be relayed. This, in fact, is often the way that these techniques function. One could say that they have their tricks: under the cover of transmitting information, their real project is to make people move, make them send things, get them to pass on or link up.[18] The anthropologist Alfonsina Bellio was witness to the same thing in one of the dreams she collected. She studies the way mediations are created around the dead in Calabria, and how, thanks to these mediations, they can take care of the living.[19] Doing this, in the context of migration breaking up communities, the dead sometimes help maintain links among people living at a great distance from each other. A young widow heard steps in the corridor at night that terrified her. Several days later, she received a call from her sister-in-law who had emigrated to a northern city: she had dreamed of her husband asking her to call his wife to tell her not to be frightened, because the steps at night in the corridor were him.[20] Dreams walk through the mouth, Tobie Nathan reminds us. That way they can travel quite a few kilometers.[21]

So in this way the dead put messages into circulation that show how they care for the living. Their gifts, the blessings that are evidence of their talents are the material to fabricate enigmas. They leave marks of their generosity, their signatures; this is enigma in the double meaning of the word: events conspire with them, and the living are intrigued. In this respect the Iceland case is exemplary. For instance, a dead person can show up, leave a message, and the dreamer often has to guess who it is meant for. If the enigma remains unsolved, it starts to circulate, until the moment when it will either be understood by someone, or reactivated by another dream or event. These apparitions can also appear when mediums are consulted. Apparitions are nets that are spread, loop by loop, to capture the "intrigued." The clearest example, given by Pons, concerns a lady called Olafur who is visited by a fairly old man during a session with a medium. The medium indicates to her that the old man is speaking a foreign language. She recognizes him; it is her grandfather, who was Norwegian. He has a friend with him who speaks the same language. Olafur recognizes him too, her grandfather's best friend, also Norwegian. There is a third person with them, also a foreigner. Olafur does not know the third person, but he bears the message. The recipient is a certain Magnusina. It is a rare Icelandic first name, but Olafur says there is an old lady in the village with that name. The medium asks if she is sick, because something is wrong. Not as far as Olafur knows; she is old, but in good health. So Olafur heads off with a double enigma: the identity of the third man and the illness. One week later, Simon, a young man in the village, learns that he has a brain tumor. He is Magnusina's grandson. Olafur goes to her place, where she learns that Simon's great-uncle had the same first name (that makes him his double protector in Icelandic tradition), and that he was Norwegian. So he was the one that Olafur met. Then Magnusina contacts Simon's parents. The messages start to circulate, and others in turn want to contact Simon's great-uncle, who might be able to send other messages via other dead people concerning other recipients. In this way, writes Pons, "the living person *a* has set off a network of relations that can be followed up beyond the relationship that she had with the living person *b,* since the circulation of her message draws in other contacts who will give other messages that will in turn go into circulation."[22] The dead are formidable enliveners. Without them, many of those who have put themselves under their protection would be less alive.

The dead also put goods into circulation, and that is the most concrete evidence of their generosity. It is in this perspective that I want to reread the transformation of this custom that consisted (and still consists) in making sure that the dead take with them one or more significant objects— significant for them or for those left behind. Here, obviously, the issue is the generosity of the living in relation to the dead. But the variations of this custom also authorize them to put themselves at the other end of the distribution chain of the goods. You will remember the Mansfield postman. In the 1940s, in certain localities of Romanian Transylvania, objects that people thought they would be in need of were sent to the defunct by the intermediary of the next to die. Sometimes even things for several people could be placed in the care of the last to go, who might find themselves with a pipe, alcohol, reading glasses, a child's toy . . .[23] It can happen that the number of objects can exceed the capacity of the coffin, so another is placed beside it. So the living make sure the dead are looking after the dead. A variation on this custom has given another use to the latter, and has stretched the network of connections between here and there: if a defunct is missing something, someone, according to this variant, has to give it to a living person who could be in need of it. These are no longer the dead in passing, but more like the dead activating links and gift exchange. Chantal Deltenre's novel *La maison de l'âme* evokes the resurgence of this practice following the massive destruction brought about by the former communist regime's systematization plan.[24] The novel's title refers to the house of the soul, a ritual whereby people who have lost a loved one offer strangers, or people passing by, shelter, food, clothing and thus keep at bay the soul of the dead (even, for those planning ahead, their very own). "You would like to see the dress you are wearing in your house up above, or even give it to a deceased close to you whom it would fit nicely. You run into a neighbor, or a stranger in your neighborhood or your building; you invite them in and offer the dress after checking that she likes it and will wear it. It is an essential condition of the gift, that it be well received."[25] Those who were victims of the systematization plan, tormented with dreams of the wandering souls of other victims who lack everything and demanding of them something to eat, to cover themselves, a roof, people who had everything taken from them, gave to others everything that the soul haunting them had need of.

Up in Iceland, the dead are also recruited in the exchange of goods and services. They are asked to take on other deceased, who, without them, would not have found a place in the cemeteries and they accompany them on their postmortem peregrinations. In fact, until the 1990s, stillborn infants could not be buried within the cemetery boundary. Not really being born, they could not have the legal status of being dead. So they were relegated to the outer limit. The solution that they had found was to confide the bodies of these infants to a simultaneous deceased, most often a stranger. Generally the family did not refuse. The request was lived through as a tribute, since these infants were only confided to "good dead," suitable people for taking the little deceased person under their protection. This practice was maintained in Reykjavík until the 1990s. At that time, the pastor, who had himself lost a stillborn infant, instaured another modality: from now on the infants would be buried at the foot of the tomb of a family member, with the status of being "hosted."[26] Inventiveness and generosity generate each other, the first being at the service of the second. And vice versa.

Some say that Iceland is not only exemplary but also fairly exceptional. It is true. As is Calabria. And Romania. Or the Toulouse area in the 1950s that Daniel Fabre was talking about. But perhaps it still is. As are plenty of other places in contemporary Europe. They are all exceptional, and thus part ways with the definition of exception. Would it not be us, in the end, who are exceptional? But obviously not very exemplary.

I'm not going to settle on that idea straightaway. No doubt, exemplarity is not everywhere the same. Difference is determined, above all, by the scale of circulations the dead are able to activate. At the places relations are cultivated, where they are inscribed into exchange mechanisms, how far one goes often proves to be vast. It proceeds, as we have seen, by extension, by a "bit by bit" that can go very far.[27] On the other hand, in those places, like with us, where suspicion reigns in a more pronounced fashion, where the maintenance of relations always runs the risk of giving rise to derision or accusations of "grieving denial," where the lady from Mansfield can make people snigger, the scale remains local. Relations are embedded in smaller communities; the capacities to feel presences are weakened, and when people, despite everything, feel "something," they have difficulty giving a meaning to what was felt. It's not the only difference. Another appears when we compare the cultural structures that frame relations. There are always mediators, in one place or another. In Iceland mediums occupy an important position. In Calabria, similar roles are taken up, mostly by women recognized for their talents. Toulouse had its "soothsayers." And in the case of Romania, the fact of knowing that they cultivate precise techniques there that allow one to summon a dead family member in one's dreams, like tearing off the right sleeve of one's shirt, not washing it, and placing it under the mattress, makes me think that there are apparatuses for framing such techniques.[28] The places where the dead take care of the living are often places occupied by or accompanied by "people who have the know-how." It is also the case with us, but there are not many such places. They are mostly little pockets resisting the discipline of mourning and rationality.

However, the generosity of the dead has no better exemplary presence with us than the possibility of organ donations.[29] It was, by the way, a book on the topic of these gifts that inspired the title of this chapter, *The Generosity of the Dead: A Sociology of Organ Procurement in France.*[30] With "procurement," the author, Graciela Nowenstein, chose not to mention "gift," for a reason. The idea of gift actually poses a problem. Nor is it by chance that in the *Dictionnaire de la mort,* there is no entry for "organ gifts," but one finds rather "organ removal" [*prélèvement d'organe*].[31] If terms like "removal" or "procurement" are preferred, it is in fact because French law chose, after 1976, to base the possibility of removal on presumed consent. In France, if you haven't stipulated the contrary, you are automatically an organ donor. Now, while it is probably the reason for the choice of these terms rather than gift, it is difficult to accept that a gift can be taken for granted. In principle, a gift is an active and personal gesture. What that means in the legal context is that from this point of view one is not giving, but allowing to take. Or, to put it less crudely, consent through silence.

The presumption of generosity has, in addition, caused quite a few problems. Legislators were obliged to revisit the law in 1990. The main problem was (and still is) the following: hospitals don't go by the law. They don't assume that presumption is enough and the medical personnel generally speak to the families and ask them what was, or would be, in their opinion, the wish of the deceased.[32] This room to maneuver that is left to the hospital teams and the families has the effect of keeping present and open the question of what the dead person wants.

This question puts the living to work. It gives them obligations. And in this way it modifies the vitality of the dead. That is how I read what the novelist Joan Didion writes in *The Year of Magical Thinking,* after the death of her husband. She accepted the autopsy, she writes, but not organ donation, because it was about his eyes.[33] In the same way, she didn't want to let go of his shoes, despite having donated all his clothes—a parenthesis here, thinking about inheritance bearing witness to the generosity of the dead, just like this incitement to generosity that translates itself into the actual distribution of his stuff.[34] What Didion calls magical thought are all these gestures, these thoughts, that leave actively open the possibility of her husband returning. And what her refusal translates is this possibility. If he comes back, what could he do without his eyes? And without his shoes? The idea of the gift, more than any other, "re-presents" the deceased. He has to be both "represented," in the sense that other people have to decide on his wishes, and he receives the chance, once again, of being made present. Sometimes, of course, in a bit of a muddle.

Organ donation again makes noticeable the particular set of actions that the dead have: they are suspended in a cascade of making-doing [*faire-faire*]. They especially make something happen to the benefiting body, something that this body was *not thought capable of doing any more*: living, pumping, purifying, and all the actions that the transplanted organ authorizes the receiving body to once again accomplish. But they make-do much more. They produce a metamorphosis, not just a transformation. Some of these people say it; they have become "other."[35]

Just questioning what the dead might want has the effect of transforming a "removal"—or even something that could look like theft[36]—into a gift. There is someone who wants to give, or who could be happy that it is done according to their wishes. Rose-Marie, the mother of a nineteen-year-old man who died from drowning, likes to say that her son saved the lives of six people, with his liver, his lungs, his kidneys, and two heart valves. "This gift that we spontaneously consented to," she writes in a letter addressed to the beneficiaries of the organ transplants from her son, "because he was so generous, has remained a posthumous tribute for him." During an interview with the psychologist Laura Perichon, the mother speaks of this extraordinary gift that "allows for travel from one life to another." And she hopes, she adds, that a reply to her letter will come to her one day with the news, as she put it, "that she has become a grandmother after all."[37]

The gift is a device that has the effect of promoting vitality among the living, the beneficiaries of the gift, and sometimes even, like Rose-Marie, among those who remain, and through whom the gift can be accomplished. But we can also hear in what she writes, and what she tells Laura, that the gift can promote vitality among the dead. Certain transplant recipients, or the family of a donor, are witness to this vitality when they say, "He is living somewhere, he understands, he sees, he is living, even if in little bits."[38] The organ prolongs the life of the deceased, just as it prolongs the life of the recipient. They inextricably become one through the other, the one with the other. Hence, speaking of the liver that she received (that she imagines is from a woman), at the moment the transplant failed and with full knowledge of what is happening, a patient will say: "She [the donor] is going to die."[39] In this perspective, we also read of the experience of a change of personality. This happened to the actor Charlotte Valandrey after a heart transplant. Her tastes changed; suddenly she liked wine and rum babas; she dreamt of memories that are not hers, about an accident, a trip to India, where she had never been; feelings of déjà-vu kept popping up. This led the actor to look for who this donor could be, and she was sure it was a woman. It led her to think that through her the donor, by saving her life, really had something added to her biography. Who knows what our hearts are capable of? "These truths will speak / through my pages, / Making your prologue— / forever mine."[40]

I cherish this idea, which can be given many meanings if it is formulated with care and read with caution, that when one being lacks life, another may share it with it.

At some point in my inquiry, Georges happened to ask for refuge in my dreams. But he did it in such a roundabout way that in order to grasp his presence, I had to learn the art of tracking coincidences.

It was at a time when I was preparing one of my first lectures on the dead. In fact, to tell the truth, I hadn't yet started preparing, but each day I was telling myself I'd better get down to it. Which is a way of preparing, although it doesn't guarantee much efficiency, and instead of reducing the anxiety, it increased it. I had just started crocheting again, making endless little chains that I was knotting together, hoping that what I wasn't managing to do with my thinking, my fingers would end up teaching me how to do.

Then the dream came.

I was in a train, a Thalys I believe, but the compartments were different from what I was used to. I was minding my own business in the train when, suddenly, I asked myself—or someone asked me, because I think I only asked myself because someone made me think of it—what I had done with my bag and my baggage, a toilet bag. Heavy feeling of uneasiness for having forgotten something somewhere and not knowing where to find it. Impotence of not knowing, not remembering, a bit of the past as if it had not taken place, like when memory breaks up, and a preceding episode is missing because the story has just begun. Someone tells me, who, I don't know, I just know that I knew him or her, they must have been in my compartment. I go there, worried. My compartment is a tiny one, with a bed, which I am not sharing with anyone, but *it doesn't lock. My bag and my toiletries are not there. I wake up very disturbed. A few steps, a drink of water. I go back to sleep shortly afterward. I go back to the train, as if I had decided to. I am once again in the little compartment. The toiletries and the bag are there.*

The following evening my son called from Lyon, where he was living. Before I spoke to him about the night before, he announces that he had a strange dream, very complicated. It began in a train, a Thalys, which was disembarking its passengers in open country. They were made to get out of the train to go into a sort of campground along the railway tracks, while waiting for the train to restart. The train didn't restart. They had to spend the night in caravans in the campground. When he woke up the next morning, no other passengers were left, only him. There were a few fairground folk working a little farther away in an alley of plane trees, like the main boulevard in our town where they put up the fairground attractions every year.

The problem, he said, was that everyone refused to speak in French or English, they were all speaking a kind of Manuš. So he had no way of knowing where he was or when the train would start again.

So he wandered around the alley, and ended up stumbling into the shop of an old Indian who suggested they shoot with a bow and arrow, which he understood would allow him to win belt buckles with eagles, the American flag, etc.

The Indian, just like the others he had met, didn't speak French or English. Seeing a banjo plectrum in his stall, Jules asked him if he spoke the language of rock; adding that he spoke it himself. So the old Indian agreed to listen to him, and took him down to the basement of his shop, in order, he had the impression, to see some monsters . . . This is when he woke up. Then, he told me, the train never started up. But, he added, it remained all the time in the background of the dream.

I tell him mine.

But then what really surprised us was when we realized next morning the date when these dreams took place. It was February 15.

We didn't interpret. We simply welcomed the idea that these dreams had nothing personal about them and that more than one person can dream them, or respond to them. As William James said of ideas, they make you think; it is dreams that make you dream.

A few days later, I received an email from my son in which he replied to my request to transcribe his dream. And at the bottom of the letter, a few lines with no obvious connection: "*Here is a little quotation that I got from a film called* Yaodong, petit traité de construction, *which is about Yaodong, houses built on the side of the mountain: 'The orientation of the tomb has consequences for the descendants. No descendants, no consequences.' I leave you,*" he concluded, "*with this thread of wool that might lead you further.*"

6
UNCERTAIN THOUGHTS

Fabulating, telling stories otherwise, is not breaking with "reality" but seeking to make it perceptible, making aspects of this reality thinkable and feel-able, aspects that are usually taken to be accessories.

—Isabelle Stengers, *La Vierge et le neutrino*

You know nothing, in the end, about the highly revolutionary power of catastrophes.

—Maud Kristen

The body of the musician Lars is stretched out on his bed. Sitting by him, his wife, Petra. With her is Heidi, a death midwife. Other people are moving about the house, including Alexa Hagerty, who is telling this story.[1] People speak in whispers, with each other and with him. Lars's mouth is wide open. As it was ever since he died a few hours ago. It is a reminder of his sickness and his agony; Lars had respiratory difficulties. The wife and the midwife attempt in vain to close his mouth. The scarf won't stay in place. They give up. They go to leave the room to take their mind off things for a moment.

When they come back, Lars's mouth is closed and he is smiling. Petra and Heidi are in agreement: it is a sign he is leaving with them. Now he is no longer suffering and is at peace.

Alexa Hagerty is a student of contemporary anthropology. Her master's thesis is about some new practices, home funerals, that have emerged in recent years in the United States. This initiative is due to a few people who got a movement together that is critical of and resisting the way in which dead bodies are treated, the commercialization of these treatments by funeral parlors, the exclusion of family, and the violence inflicted on the body through embalming techniques. These collectives decided to relearn how to take care of the dead and share their expertise. Thus trained, the advisers deal with administrative and legal issues, help look after the bodies, check decomposition, and organize the wake. They are called "death midwives," or doulas.

These wakes are their main focus of attention. The dead bodies are no longer inert objects, but keep their status as persons. You have to continue speaking to them, *softly, with love, choosing the words with care,* because, the midwives tell us, if we have to get used to seeing them go, the dead themselves have to get used to it, and we have to help them in this. Death is no longer inscribed in medicoscientific temporality, it is no longer something that arrives at a determined moment (and especially as determined by doctors), it becomes a longer process in which what is called the "agency" of the person, their capacity to act, remains "vibrant" as Hagerty says, precisely because communication remains possible.

And that is indeed how Lars's smile was understood, as a sign. But who makes the sign? A sign is always the product of a connection, an active liaison between beings and things. But in this context it takes on a partic-ular meaning: a sign is the product of events conspiring together. It is not defined by its origin, which can remain indeterminate—its determination guarantees nothing—but it needs a recipient, because a sign makes sense only if it is has an addressee. It solicits an interpreter, or, more precisely, it interpellates. This means the interpreter is not expected to interpret, just act. The sign translates as well as it activates the vitality of the relations between the living and the dead.

The midwife and Petra are in agreement on the fact that Lars's smile is a sign. It comforts his wife and his family. Saying it like that is paying attention to effects. More precisely, it is taking care of events in their ef-fects. No one is obliged to take it further—this "it" that comforts, who is it, what is it? But you could, if you wanted. For example, you could suggest that Lars has given a sign to his family by smiling. Those who cultivate the practice of home funerals would accept this without a problem, or even say it, given that they think death does not interrupt the process of life; cells continue to communicate for some time, hair grows, the body transforms. This conception could, by enlarging the temporal space in which it is situated, allow for some truth to what the physiologist Xavier Bichat proposed at the end of the eighteenth century when he stated that a dying man "dies bit by bit."[2] He slowly disappears from the world to the extent that the senses wane, sight weakens, hearing perceives only certain sounds, just as odors only leave a faint impression. What do we know of the body's capacities to feel after it stops breathing?

The death midwives share the conviction that death is not a matter of all or nothing. The heart may have stopped beating, but there is still someone, a kind of presence, although of course much reduced. They have the hypothesis that the dead continue to understand and even reply to the words of the living, and the question of care is not the sole resort of the latter. The dead can reply by way of facial expressions, odors, or even via signs in nature or the immediate environment. They can still speak with those who remain, through their memories or through thoughts that arrive in their presence.[3] These are signs, and as such, remain open to the possibility of being understood differently. Lars smiles to comfort his family, and the midwife, like the widow, interprets it like that.

But she also adds that death can, as it happens, modify the musculature of their face in such a way as to produce a postmortem smile. Yet, adds Hagerty, one explanation does not block the other. The midwife adds a possibility, not in an "either/or" kind of way, but in a "but also" mode, the precious grammatical register of conjunctions: and, and, and . . .

This deliberate coexistence requires a particular type of epistemological engagement that the home funeral people call the "threshold." The threshold, Hagerty writes "is the space at the heart of which the smile of a dead man is both a muscular movement *and* a supernatural communication, a space at the heart of which the body is both biological *and* sacred, object *and* subject, disenchanted *and* enchanted, inert *and* still offering its *enspirited* care."

The disjunctive and polemical "either/ors" of mainstream conceptions are carefully replaced by "ands," and it is these "ands" that challenge medical epistemology. Because, unlike the latter, the home funerals arrangement considers that each version "adds" to the situation rather than forcing a subtraction in favor of another. The fact that the smile can be a "natural" phenomenon did not stop Lars from being able to want to comfort his family. It is not hypotheses of enchantment that contest medical epistemology; it is the affirmation of the possibility of the coexistence of multiple and contradictory versions. The "and" introduces a nonpolemical contestation. I would say it is an *open* contestation (in the sense that it opens onto other narrations), in terms of "there is always something else." It's an engagement to the extent that it transforms ways of thinking and feeling. It implies a way of getting into a similar kind of relation to the one the anthropologist Tanya Luhrmann observed among evangelical Christians who learn to pray in order to communicate with God, which she theorizes as "a third type of epistemological commitment: not materially real like tables and chairs, not fictional like Snow White and the Seven Dwarf, but a different conceptual space, defined by the constant necessity to suspend disbelief, and in so doing, by the awareness that doubt is probable."[4]

For people experimenting with these living relationships with God, this commitment requires them to develop another way of relating to the world. They learn to modify the perceptions and ways of thinking with which we usually function. We have learned, at least in our cultures, to think of there being a tight membrane, a barrier between the exterior world, including the consciousnesses of others, and our own minds [*esprit*]. We can infer what others might have in their heads, but we know that these contents are private. Others are not *in* our heads, and we are not *in* theirs. Consciousnesses are separate, though one can, observing how others are acting, guess what they are thinking or what their intentions might be. This is known to psychology as "having a theory of mind." It is what produces the feeling that the source of our thought is coming from us, that these are "our" thoughts that are in our heads and not in others'. And we live with the conviction that the events of the world happen relatively independently of intentions. We learn how to tell the difference between a song that we play in our head and one we hear on the radio. We learn how to distinguish between what we think and what we perceive. And we do not think, for example (still following the theory of mind), that the fact of seeing a spider is the result of any particular intention, except that of the spider being there; the fact that it is there at the same time we are hangs on chance. So hearing God reply to you in a conversation requires breaking with this "theory of mind"; it requires a kind of unlearning of habits.[5] Hearing God speak to you in your thoughts, hearing him reply to your questions or to the demands that you address to him, presupposes accepting that other thoughts can come into your own, without you being at the origin of them. Similarly, seeing certain worldly events, for example, finding a parking place or a hundred-euro bill on the pavement, just when you asked God to come to your aid, as if they were concrete responses he was bringing you, also presupposes that you have broken with the theory of mind. This requires the capacity to hear others think in you and to translate events as intentions and to recognize, to discriminate, when that happens. It is a technique, and it is acquired. It is an expertise and it has a name: the porous mind.

Understanding Lars's smile as an intentional act is evidence of a competence that is similar to the porous mind, as is welcoming certain events as signs, that is, as indicators of intentions, or the organization of events by a thought. There is thought elsewhere than in our heads. There is an "it thinks" in the world of events. This would be the first dimension of signs: they translate a different distribution of intentions and application of thought. On this basis, they put thought to work.

As I was drafting these lines, I had an email from Félicianne Ledoyen, a lady who often sends me stories mingling the resourceful lives of her cats with the equally rich lives of her departed. Her letter began like this: "One might think some events we go through that still leave us perplexed years afterwards to be 'by chance.' "[6] This is a quite pragmatic way to define signs, that is, by their effects. They bring about perplexity. In that respect they belong to the family of enigmas, perhaps as their closest relatives. Once they have made a sign, they keep the thought alive. "It thinks" spreads out.

Alexa Hagerty relates that during the three days' wake with Carol's corpse, several people saw a spider. The first appeared late at night, just as the midwife finished tending to the body. As she was leaving the house, she noticed it again on the stoop. The animal came back again, several times. It was seen at the burial, during the lowering of the coffin, an enormous spider following it at the same rate on its invisible thread. "The phrase 'Carol was a spider' enmeshes us," writes Hagerty, "in a web of signification. 'Carol was a spider' can be understood as a statement of fact or metaphor. Or both."[7] One. Or the other. Oscillating, vacillating, triggering impulses, departing from a balancing point that is created in movement, and holds us. *Walk the line,* as they say in English.

The sociologist Jérémy Damian has taken up this "walking the line" when he tries to give an account of the experience of dancers in dance contact improvisation. As he strives to find the right way to talk about it, he writes "walk the line" when "what is at issue is to hold the ridge line between two worlds that meet badly or damage each other; the positivist one, and the sensory experience one often turning too fast, on request, in romantic lyrical flights . . . 'walk the line, buddy!' Hold the line, don't fall. . . . David Abram balancing across two voids when he suggests doing without the category of the supernatural and announces he is less interested in the 'literal' truth of his statements and more by the type of relationships they make possible, hold the line, even if on several occasions he is caught vacillating. Perhaps he is the one who in the end put me on the path of a discourse that does not have as its aim the description or explanation of an experience, but rather the aim of giving it a form that produces what it is describing, that stimulates a transformation in our ways of feeling."[8]

Here Damian touches on something important. Writing so as not to explain but to change relations, ways of relating. Vacillating writing. This is how I could understand what the midwife Heidi is doing when she suggests to Petra "that [referring to the postmortem smile of Petra's husband, Lars] could just as easily be a biological phenomenon that we have learned to recognize in the changes due to death" and doing it after having been through, with her, the possible version of a sign addressed by Lars. What Heidi does is not explain, and even less rationalize; it is to act on ways of thinking and feeling. This is cultivating the art of moving from one world to another without tipping, or, to use another image, making heterogeneous, and normally contradictory, ways of thinking and feeling communicate and inscribe them in new relationships. It is learning to make things coexist. This is the difficult exercise that signs are calling for.

Sunday, November 6, 1955, the actor Anny Duperey and her sister lost their parents. The actor was eight at the time, the younger sister still in the crib. Duperey will write two books on the subject, *Le voile noir* and then *Je vous écris*, which collects the letters that were sent to her. In the second book she relates that every anniversary, each November 6, was a very difficult moment for her sister. On the eve of one of these anniversaries, when they were adults, her sister had a dream. She was in a big bookstore and in the middle were two coffins, their parents'. Everyone looked like this was normal; it was a very peaceful atmosphere in the bookshop. This dream can, of course, be interpreted, and Duperey does so. Her first book, *Le voile noir*, had been out on the shelves for several months, so since that time the dead parents had been exposed. The next day, as her sister wasn't too well, her husband suggested she treat herself, and, since she had dreamt of a bookstore, to go and buy herself a book. Her mood being rather dark, she chose a light read, a detective novel. She settled on a Simenon because the black humor of the title appealed to her: *En cas de malheur* [*In Case of Adversity*]. She left, perked up by the irony of the title. Starting to read it when she got home, she came upon the title of the first chapter: "Sunday, November 6." There can't be too many Sunday November 6s; then she saw on the title page that the novel was written and published in 1955. "By the time she got to my place," writes Duperey, "my sister was still in a state of shock, and she brandished the book in my face, tapping on the chapter title and title page with a trembling finger." Both were stunned. Then, her sister asked her in a somewhat anguished voice, "But what about you, do you BELIEVE it?" "Do I believe . . . I'd certainly like to," writes the author, "be a person of faith. It must be a comfort. But unfortunately I believe myself to have more of a temperament tending to doubt. It is always there to moderate any flightiness, put a brake on my beliefs. But, after all, doubt can keep good company with my inner smile that comes up in circumstances like that. I discover it. We so want to believe that our loved ones are there with us, that we don't dare believe it. We doubt, and yet we already believe it. The idea is neither more distressing, nor more reassuring—*it is*." Duperey goes on to say that she "told this story to her friend Maurice. And I said to him—being really careful about it—if we admit that our dead, our parents, had wanted to give us a sign, their chosen method looks almost like a joke. Doing it via a crime novel, that's not the way respectable dead people should behave! He looked at me for a moment before replying, without laughing, 'Really? And why would the living have a monopoly on humor?' "[9]

Andrée, who was interviewed by Laura Perichon, told the story that at her father's burial, a glass had literally exploded in the hand of one of her uncles. They said to themselves, "That's one of dad's tricks.' But two years later, when their mother died, the same thing happened again. "That," she said, "gave me something to think about, saying to myself, what's going on here? It is as if he were injecting a bit of fun into something heavy and difficult."[10]

Signs take us by surprise. They are the unexpected on the surface of routine, as Marcos Mateos says.[11] That is where their humor lies. Signs all have humor in one form of another. That is how they are able to surprise us. The very act of making a sign is a kind of humor, as it transgresses the order of things. They communicate things that normally remain disconnected, through the strangest of systems of affinities, the grandiose and the derisory, the serious and the comic, the banal and the sacred. They are resourceful in their divergences: they use biological mechanisms in order to console; they divert the flow of electricity to make an appearance; they use crime fiction to make dates coincide. They create dramatic scenes in mischievous bad taste. They misuse metamorphoses and thwart the symbolic, which is none of their business: they refer to things other than themselves—the spider is thus about Carol—that is, to themselves becoming something else (one can become a spider when one is dead). They also use, and this is their special privilege, the technique of repetition, as in comic movies, because repetition is the most habitual mode of being— spiders, "hey, there it is again"; as is resemblance, semantic resemblance (the troglodyte and the wren, for those who read Félicianne's story that I cite in note 6), or formal resemblance, or something else that makes us say, "This is not just random." Insistence is their way of being. They surprise us with their insistence; it is a technique, their technique. It makes up for their intrinsic weakness that is the allusive regime of signs; it can only proceed by way of allusion or derivation. So signs are not exactly of the same order as interpellation; they relate to a more interruptive [*apostrophe*] form of interpellation. They turn around to interpellate you from a distance. They make things bifurcate. They make things break out of their habits, because, as we know, things have habits—but often we only discover them when they deviate. The things no longer carry the same signification, now they are *signing*.

Repetition, insistence, deviation. Nanou relates that on the anniversary of a lovely trip she took awhile back with her now deceased husband, and at the same place of that trip, she is with her daughter and buys herself some earrings, then has second thoughts. They were really too expensive. Her daughter tells her to buy a lottery ticket; the coincidence of the dates and the place make it worth trying for other coincidences. The winning prize is exactly the amount the jewelry cost. As if he wanted, Nanou says, to give her a present. Was it the dead man who intervened? Are people particularly disposed to understand them when dates and places coincide? Are signs fabricated to allow for this availability? Nanou herself translates the plural possibilities of this story when she says, "I am sensitive to certain things in which I can discern the presence of my husband, or more precisely, the vitality of our story in my life today."[12] Signs proceed by way of intensification.

People think that signs, when they don't frighten us, make us happy because they make contact with the missing. It is not false, but it remains very partial. What signs do is substantiate, while creating, out of another relationship to the world, a rupture in this relationship, in order to instaure nonhabitual connections; Nanou sensitizes herself to something that can generate another way of feeling. And the world becomes imaginative. Or rather, its power to imagine, its vitality, suddenly becomes apparent to us. Signs are sensational. On the quiet.

Two years ago, when I was having breakfast in the restaurant of the hotel where I was staying in Paris, and I was discussing the progress of my project with a few girlfriends, a lady whom I hadn't noticed came up just as we were rising from the table. She apologized for the disturbance, but hadn't been able to stop herself from overhearing our conversation. She had lost her husband the year before, and was looking for things to read that might help her. After I got home, I sent her a list. She wrote to thank me, closing with these words, "I can't help but think that it is perhaps not by chance that we crossed paths that day, especially since I also am from Liège." Chance weaves a succession of coincidences: and, and, and. *And* we are in the same hotel (by chance), *and* we are attached through the dead (by chance), *and* we are Liégeoises. Another email came a few days later to thank me again, but I think more to prolong or complete the sequence: ". . . and I want to thank you all the more for having taken the time to reply to me, since I went online and I saw that you are very busy, and that in addition you work on animals, and I am passionate about them." *And, and, and.* When a sign comes to you, says the sociologist Benedikte Zitouni, "as a contraction, a sudden and unpredictable coming together of the world in one point that makes you sensitive to other connections."[13] You were speaking of someone who had died, when, coming out of the open window of a passing car is "your song" as a couple, a blackbird lands two paces away, and unexpected snow beings to fall. Contraction, consistency in a point that makes each of these elements vibrate together as if reality were making itself felt. Here where separations are usually produced, the classification system is lifted, and things begin to communicate differently. This creation of consistency is new pleats forming that create new relationships for things, or rather make things that were otherwise separated, and without prior connection, "relate to each other."

Lastly, signs function in a mode of complicity, or collusion. In their relationship with each other, as we have seen, but no one will be left out. They need the collusion of those they are addressing; they are on a quest for accomplices, readers, attentive semiologists, dreamers. In many cases this complicity is also the basis for their weakness. First because the accusation that they are the mere products of subjectivity still weighs on them: "Signs only say what you want to make them to say." You think you are the recipient, but you are the sender. You say you are the reader, but you are the author. Your writing is recognized. Caught in the act of colluding. Above all: tragic misunderstanding. If you read the above carefully, none of those welcoming signs is blind to this possibility. Quite the contrary. The acceptance of a sign is made in the realm of "perhaps," of doubt, of "I couldn't stop myself from thinking" (so there is a possible "thinking otherwise"), of "as ifs," of rephrasings. Each of these nuances, these restarts, these moderations of the power of signs, these "maybes" is evidence of the fact that these people fabricate their experiences with the very material of coexistence; a cloth with holes, multicolored and never hemmed, in its plurality of versions. Each "perhaps," each "as if," every doubt expressed, every new beginning "in other words," mobilizes implicit "ands" and eager "but thens" in search of another version.

It is first of all here—this will be the subject of the last chapter—that lies the great intelligence that I discovered listening to people tell me their stories, the amazing intelligence of the crafting [mise en récit] of their experiences. Then, that vulnerability that the sign knows when it is faced with the accusation that it depends on the person recognizing it as a sign, comes from our not having a lexicon, a dictionary, a system of recognition or conversion. No translation techniques. We haven't sufficiently cultivated this kind of thing to know how to build up a common knowledge. These practices are not frames; that makes them very vulnerable, both to the accusation of irrationality that is always a threat, and equally to the poverty of responses that are culturally open to the question, "What do we do with that?," and also to the possibility of checking up on signs, that is to say, an art of discrimination; anything can, from one moment to the next, make a sign.[14] So, there is not much left hanging on.[15]

Louis Isebald Petre was born in Vilvoorde on June 17, 1892. On February 15, 1904, at the time of the accident, he was only eleven years old. His father was called Antoine; his mother, Louise. He had two brothers, a little younger than he, Jules and Henri. Antoine and Louise lived long lives. They did not die until much later, 1935 for him, 1941 for her. She was seventy-eight years old; he was eighty. I finally found their genealogy. The accent had to be removed: it was Petre, not Pètre.

But what I learn from the family trees confounds my story—because my father's cousin was right about the dates. Joseph died in 1909, on November 4 exactly. And Bertha, two months and eighteen days later, on January 22, 1910. They lived for another five years. Five years, time to give birth to Ghislaine and see her grow a little. At the time of Georges's death, Bertha was two months pregnant.

But what would they have died of then? He was not yet fifty years old; she was only forty-eight. My friend Jean-Marc tells me that "dying of grief" was a term used euphemistically to speak of the Spanish flu. His uncle, he told me, "died of grief" following the loss of his twin. This epidemic caused nearly twenty million deaths. But it did not happen until after the war. Georges's parents died before they could die of many other things. As if they had jumped at the first opportunity.

What happened to them? Can dying of sadness be postponed? And if that's not it, why would she go so quickly after him? Could Joseph and Bertha have been victims of the flu of sorrow?

What has really changed between the destinies of Antoine and Louise, Joseph and Bertha? I will never know. I do not know the fate of Louis's parents. I do not know how they lived, or whether they were able to find joy again. I don't know if they were talking about Louis, among themselves or with others, or how they answered questions from Jules and Henri. I also don't know if Jules and Henri talked about Louis to their own children. And if the children of these knew of his existence, or if one of these children looks like him, passing on to the next generation a part of his life or how he looked. We sometimes see gestures, a tic, a sense of humor, appearing in heirs who may not have known their antecedents, the very ones who were rehearsing, without knowing it, what they were going to become in the life of another.

But the fact remains that the stories told by my father and his cousin are similar. The cousin was mistaken about the date of Georges's death, my father about that of the parents. But in that way they both preserved the same story differently, that of an indisputable link between the two events. And that's what matters. This is the story I inherited. The one that reminds me of Georges and his parents' grief.

7

PUTTING OUR TRUST IN SPIRITS

How to Call on Them

The dialogue with the dead should never be broken before
they deliver, from the future, that which is buried with
them.

—Heiner Müller

Let it go. Let it finish. Give consciousness a holiday. Quit
the annoying habit of doing everything by yourself. Instead,
the important thing (in the order of thought) is always to
leave it unfinished. Wait for one's light. Sacrifice the first
man who makes us live wounded lives. Make the daïmon
return. Reestablish relations.

—Henri Michaux, *Connaissance par les gouffres*

Christophe Pons tells us that in Iceland, when a child is frightened by the
presence of a dead person who comes to visit him or her at night, the child
is advised to ask him or her who they are and what they want. Very often
this puts an end to these untimely visits. They know what to do. Putting
that more concretely, they don't interpret, they experiment.

During a conversation, Helga talks to him about her son-in-law whom
she loved very much. "Jón was nice," she said. "He was a lovely man. He
always did the right thing with his boys. I think he is not entirely gone. I
often have the feeling that Jón is here among us! It is hard to explain. . . .
For example, when I babysit my grandchildren at my daughter's place, I
feel his presence in the room; he is there. I feel it because it isn't the same
atmosphere. I don't know how to explain it, it is a good impression, a
good atmosphere, and after a few moments I understand that it is him. I
say to myself, 'Ah, it's only Jón.' That happened to me the last time. I felt
he was there. He was there standing beside me, he was smiling looking
at his boys. . . . He was wearing brown clothing, and he would have been
ready to return if he could have." Referring to her allusion to the color of

his suit, Pons then asked her, "But you saw him?" And she replies, "No, no, I didn't see anything, but I felt he was there."[1] Pons identifies the paradox: she recognizes an image that she cannot see. And she was able to "see" because what she "saw" takes on meaning in Iceland: brown clothes indicate that the dead person is well, that he is peaceful. This visit is part of what Pons calls "specific experimental modalities," which allow one to understand and transmit them. In other words, the experiments are framed.

The lack of a code labeling our own relationships with the dead, and with signs, does not make the situations any less interesting; it makes them more difficult, more dangerous, and more vulnerable—for example, to stupidity. They don't give rise to trust. And trust, in this area, is vital.

I had mentioned, when I was thinking about the different possibilities for the dead to manifest their generosity in regard to the living, that these manifestations could be limited by the absence of mediators. But I also announced that places can still be found where these mediations exist, places where good ways of addressing and generating messages are cultivated, and where, above all, trust is put in signs. These are spiritualist circles.[2]

The séance of November 21, 2010, the first I attended, begins at 10:00 a.m. precisely in a small comfortable room with subdued lighting. A conference table is set up on a stage in front of the audience. Just next to the stage, at the level of the audience, two ladies are seated at another table, face-to-face at either end, perpendicular to the room. These are the secretaries; they will be taking notes of each message transmitted by the clairvoyant and they will give them to the people concerned at the end of the séance. At least thirty people, of all ages, men and women, have come along. Two ladies, the two mediums, surround the officiator, who opens the séance with a prayer from Allan Kardec's spiritualist gospel. The text of the day speaks of the ingratitude of the living, especially that of certain children in relation to their parents. After this reading, the officiator explains one of the foundations of spiritualism to us: before being reincarnated, the soul has to acknowledge its errors and the suffering occasioned by others. Certain souls can decide to be reincarnated next to the spirit that made them suffer, and they should learn to love it. All souls should take stock of the preceding terrestrial incarnation and recognize their errors. One of the difficulties for them is learning to pardon and to quit their hatred, because resentment risks following them into their future life.

Michèle, the first clairvoyant, is a lady of about sixty and she begins the séance with a brief introduction, a sort of secular sermon, even if it repeats a part of the text from the gospel that had just been read. She speaks with her gaze fixed on a photograph hanging on the wall. It is a photo of Frère Clément, a medium who died a long time ago, but who guides her at each séance.

Some members of the audience have left photos of their deceased at the entrance. At the moment they are in an envelope on the table. Michèle takes a photo and concentrates on it. The officiator reminds us that we should only respond with "yes," "no," or "I don't know." "What will be said to us," he adds, "are not orders, but advice that the dead give us. We have the choice to follow this advice, but not all the dead have the same wisdom. If you do not recognize the person visiting us, or you don't understand what they are saying, this will perhaps make sense when you go home, or later on."

There is an abundance of histories of spiritualist movements. I won't take them up here; that is not what I'm about. What I am interested in is the whole apparatus. What is it doing? More importantly, what is it making-doing? One aspect of this story, however, deserves mentioning, because it is still cultivated in séances. The spiritualist movement is a resistive apparatus. It was historically; first in relation to religious institutions, but also to scientific positivism. The historian Jay Winter has an interesting comparison with apparitions of the Virgin Mary in popular religion. These apparitions were able to constitute an indictment against the indifference and remoteness of the clergy. In fact, in 1871, a year after the First Vatican Council had proclaimed the doctrine of papal infallibility, five children of peasant background, in Pontmain in the west of France, saw the Virgin and received her message. In other words, "a group of *ordinary* children beat a path toward the divine, and the divine comes to them."[3] The spiritualist movement can be subjected to a similar reading. Not only will its doctrine contradict a number of church dogmas, but it also will encourage practices that the church disapproves of, notably unregulated contact with the dead. But this isn't the only motive for resistance. Today the spiritualist movement translates, as do home funerals, a resistance to dominant psychological theories of personhood and mourning. Alexa Hagerty explains that the ideas cultivated by the midwives of death disrupt the "model of a singular bounded individual mind. Importantly, [they] also challenge ideas about grief that emerge from such a model, namely the Freudian imperative to withdraw object cathexes from the lost object. This sense of the danger of mourning slipping into melancholia is seen in the everyday encouragements offered to mourners (and made explicit on commercial sympathy cards) to 'move through' grief and 'get over' loss. Home funerals offer a model of grief in which it is not something to get over, but to *cultivate*."[4]

Spiritualist practices prove to be close to these notions of resistance.[5] On the one hand, the theory of mind underpinning the movement also breaks with the dominant theories. On the other, mourning, like the ideas of the midwives, has nothing to do with rupture, but more with looking after and intensifying relations, processes in which dead are actively implicated.

The break with the theory of mind operates, first of all, through the medium's practice. She is inhabited by another being whose intentions she conveys. There is someone speaking in her and who makes her speak. She attests to an experience that puts into motion the kind of porosity of the soul that Luhrmann speaks of, and she leads that experience to its limits. Next, the medium never stops exploring what the anthropologist Maurice Bloch calls *breaches in the opposition between being and nonbeing,* and he doubles up, not only in summoning a dead person, making it pass from nonbeing to being, but in situating himself in these breaches, in such a way that his person has to efface itself in order to let the dead "act."[6] So it is no surprise that many mediums have been subjected to accusations of hysteria or other diagnoses of mental issues. They are living contradictions of what, according to the norm, defines the psyche and the acceptable repertoire of its faculties. This is what I learned by going to séances: mediums cultivate a quite different way of thinking and feeling.

So, when Michèle the clairvoyant tells a person whose father has just manifested, "I don't know what he is referring to, I don't understand what he means, but he says that you will understand," she is making it clear that she is inhabited by another being, that she is no longer speaking, the proof being that she doesn't understand what she is saying. In stating that she does not have access to the meaning of the message, she endorses the success of the presentification:[7] Not only does the dead have a presence, but he also actively "presents himself" by the very fact of this presence effacing the medium's. Without her, of course, the dead couldn't manifest himself; it is through her voice that he can speak, through her capacity to hear that he can transmit things. But what he has to say, and what she doesn't understand, no longer springs from the medium, it is a matter between him and his recipient. Michèle endorses the intimacy of the relationship precisely through her explicit self-exclusion. She creates a kind of collusion between the defunct and the person he is coming to see: "It's your story now, this is between you." At the same time she harnesses the latter with the work of resolving a series of enigmas: what does the dead person want to tell? What does he mean to me? Is it really he?

The interior limits of the participants themselves are equally subject to some less radical redefinition. For example, I heard an amazing piece of advice given to a young woman. Her "visiting" grandmother tells us that she knows of many conflicts with her mother. This grandmother tells her through the intermediary of Michèle, "You cannot speak to her when you are with her, that is pointless. But, when you go to sleep, and she is sleeping in the bedroom next to you, speak to her in her head." This is said with the unambiguous condition that in this way the message could finally be understood. This injunction broadens the conception of how the consciousnesses of the dead and the living "communicate"—in the most literal sense—since it extends the possibility to the living. So, even more porosity of the soul. Capacities for feeling are amplified; variations in ways of being present are explored.

This redefinition of the limits of interiority can equally take the form of an actual induction when Michèle invites an adolescent to cultivate what might be the first stirrings of a talent as a medium. Following a visit from his grandfather in the course of a séance (where she will specify that he is accompanied by a gentleman who rolls his r's), she asks him if sometimes he "has the impression that there is a kind of presence." She reassures him: "This is often the case with all small children, who are often still a bit on the other side, and who say: 'There is someone.' And it comes back very strongly at the stage of puberty." In doing this the clairvoyant normalizes the experience, but without making it banal. She locates it both in the everyday world, the one children grow up in, and she is witness at the same time to another world, that of the other side, where sometimes they can still have one foot. Then Michèle invites the adolescent to intensify his capacity for feeling presences. She asks him if he listens to contemporary music at high volume. He nods again. She says to him: "You need silence in order to hear." She advises him to leave his radio on, but muted, in that way his grandfather can talk to him. She concludes: "It is a wonderful gift, being a medium, but it is a two-edged sword. The lower astral is there [what the Icelanders themselves express when they say, "You never know which dead person you will come across"]. I don't think you pray much, but if you try to [make contact], then pray beforehand. Obviously they trust you, that's probably why they sent your grandfather to you."

These few extracts already give an overview of everything that happens in a séance and the formidable technical arsenal that is brought to bear. The spiritualist movement is an apparatus that takes care of the dead *and* the living, and does so in the most ecological, most organized way; it delegates to some the care of others, and vice versa. In this perspective, it is a therapeutic apparatus. It is often stressed that spiritualist practices have a consoling value. They had it, and they still have it. Not only does the vision on which they are based form a promise to find those we love, but it also allows individuals to hope for a postmortem future that is a little less dark than nothingness with, moreover, the possibility of progress. This is reflected in the central statement of the Allan Kardec doctrine: "To be born, to die, to be reborn and to continually progress, such is the law." But the comforting dimension is only one dimension of these practices. First, they were from their origin, according to Christine Bergé's suggestion, a "pedagogy of pain, an education in mourning," not as the psychiatry of the time had it, a pathology of pain.[8] Then they offered an original response to the experiences that those who were becoming mediums were living through.

What the spiritualist movement does, writes Bergé, is "to understand and socialize pain" by refusing to lock it inside the suffering individual, the medium in this case. They are now conceived of as "sensuous inter-

preters" of the world of pain and of evil.[9] Bergé places this care system in
the context of its emergence in Lyon in the second half of the nineteenth
century. Faced with the development of the rational, efficient industrial
machine, "these mentally ill patients, whom Charcot will call ambulatory
automata, are spreading dangerously." These are wandering sleepwalkers,
dispossessed of will, moved by incomprehensible forces that an alarmed
psychology will try, wherever possible, to return to reason. Spiritualism
will find a completely different and much more original solution: this
"other who has my desire" designates a particular talent that it is a question
of channeling or domesticating. Spiritualism "educates the sleepwalker,
guides the automaton. Mediums are nothing other than channeled beings,
subdued automata," taken by Spirits wishing to communicate. Spiritualism
offers "a new and recognized vocation to mediums whose sometimes
marginal or even pathological character would have led them to the psychiatric hospital."[10] We note that it is typically the case that mediums find
this path after terrible ordeals in life—this is the case for Michèle, as well as
her son who is taking over from her. These mournings, these illnesses, in
which life and death questions are replayed, are all experiments leading the
mediums to the brink of these breaches of the opposition between being
and nonbeing. Michèle herself says it even more precisely: "Mediums are
people who are neither in the world of the living nor in the world of the
dead, but who have one foot in both." Affinities, proximity, intimacy, above
all with those "no longer being," that is to say "being otherwise." These
are, says Bergé, elective signs: grief, illness, pain are all ways of appealing.

Christophe Pons noted, in his own research in Iceland, that one cannot
fail, by listening to the different messages transmitted by the deceased,
to be struck by their extreme banality. It's exactly the feeling that everyone I've been with has had. The dead often don't say much. They most
often give encouragement or advice: "You should take a little more care
of yourself"; "People love you and you don't believe them"; "You need
to have more confidence in yourself." They don't say much but they do
things. Or, rather, they activate, they make do [font faire].

The dead are raised again. They commit to refabricating the past in the
present. This will be the case, for example, when the message is organized
around grudges and resentment. Often there is something that remains be

done, has not been said, or not been understood. Death does not prevent the resolution of unresolved conflicts. Quite the contrary. The dead take an active part that they could not take on board when they were alive. Sometimes they explain themselves, but they are always actively coming to ask the living to forgive them. They also always transmit their affection. There is a benevolent atmosphere, good-natured at times; the serious and the flippant rub shoulders. Certainly there are moments of deep sadness. And moments of humor. We laugh, sometimes, and good-heartedly. We can even make fun of the dead. Michèle said to a lady, "She was your mother-in-law; she loved you very much." "I don't know." "What do you mean! I am shocked! You didn't know she loved you!? Now she is angry." Michèle calms down. Then, with a smile: "She wasn't good at housework, was she? Work wasn't her thing, not like you." Undaunted, the lady replies: "I'm not saying bad things about the dead." The audience laughs. But behind the apparent flippancy, there is something going on, which one can guess at even without knowing much about what it is with this lady and her mother-in-law. One might be right to think that Michèle is "doing" something; she is already in the process of registering the relationship in two modes: first, that of reconstructing history by imposing the point of view of the mother-in-law, then, with the criticism that she addresses her with, she forces the daughter-in-law to situate herself in this relationship. Michèle opens up the possibility of creating a distance, a space for conflict; the challenge of the talents of housewife could be read as the opening of a practicable conflict that will allow them to take up other lesser ones.[11] The daughter-in-law, in fact, does not refuse this offer when she comes up with the cliché, "One should not speak ill of the dead." On the contrary, she reinforces it when she asserts that it is the codes of civility with regard to the deceased that prohibit her from saying it. The clairvoyant creates the parameters for the relationship and, by situating these in a possibly conflicted space, seeks to figure out what the lady is coming to ask for.

When, on another occasion, she introduces a father's message to his daughter with these words, I understand it in the same way: "He is your father, is he not?" At the nod, she continues, looking at her carefully: "He didn't love you." She leaves a moment of silence; the daughter doesn't react. So she resumes, more assertively: "He loved you very much." Then she describes the father, talks about his infectious laugh and his kindness, about his love of life; he stopped smoking and drinking at one point. But it was harder to stop drinking. Was he an actor? I see him on a stage. Comic theater. He liked a laugh. He liked a good joke. *I was happy.* (Michèle goes from narration to direct speech, without transition.) He was a good man. She expresses his regrets for giving so much anxiety to his relatives. *I made you worry so much! I'm sorry now.* She then repeats the love he felt for his daughter and brings up the question of her projects, in which he supported her. Perhaps this father's love for his daughter was ambivalent? Over the course of a lifetime, you can have a lot of love at times, less at others. Who knows? But we can see something else here. We can read the first of the two propositions as bait, as a way of asking: "What are you coming for?"; "What do you want with him?"; "What are you coming to resolve?" We understand, following the girl's lack of reaction, that her father's love was not the issue she came to settle. And we can still see other possible stories there. And, and, and . . .

Michèle addresses a man in his forties, in a reproachful tone of voice. His wife is there, she says. She's not doing too well. "It seems you are wallowing in misfortune." He exclaims: "Wallow in misfortune! You can ask her all about that!" Everybody laughs. Michèle continues: "But you are making your wife unhappy; your wife is feeling guilty. You can't blame the dead. It is not their fault for leaving; it was their time, you can't do anything about it. And your wife feels guilty because you make her guilty." Then she continues: "Your grandfather is also there behind you, with his hand on your shoulder." This is a regular feature, always physically locating the dead. He is behind you, next to you, hand on your shoulder. In fact, it is always doubled up, from a spatial point of view, as we have just seen, and from a spatiotemporal point of view. They are localized in an evolution by an ascending geo-ontology; it rises or remains stagnant, and this changes its status, its regime of existence and presence.[12] From this double assignment of a place and a place in time that determines his state, his "way of being," the dead is both present in the present and inscribed in a long temporality: the past that we evoke with him, the present of his presence and his status, the future that is sketched out by that ascent.

What also appears in the exchange that has just occurred is a subtle variation of mourning theory. It is not a question of detaching oneself from the dead to reinvest in other objects, to "get out from under the yoke" as some say. No, it's the dead woman who's asking to be released here. Remember the jars heavy with tears, the sack hindering the race, the little schemes of desire, the dead's concern for the living. The question of guilt is also replayed; it is she, the deceased, who feels guilty, unjustly. Many of those who have lost someone know the dreaded work of the remorse-making machine that death sets up in you without your asking. We didn't take the time; we got annoyed too quickly because he was getting old or she was getting sick; we didn't say goodbye; we weren't there when needed; we got irritated; we didn't say we loved her. In these séances, the guilt never stops being displaced, replayed, redistributed. It takes many forms. Now it's the dead who didn't say or do the right thing, and he's the one who didn't say goodbye. He knew we loved him. And he's the one who comes to ask for forgiveness. We do not know *what* we are losing, wrote psychoanalyst Jean-Bertrand Pontalis.[13] But not *all* is lost.

The methods of bringing people into each other's presence are carefully constructed. The beginning of the message often begins with a "he is telling me that . . . ," accompanied by the greeting of the person to whom this message is addressed. Direct speech gradually takes over, indicated in French by the familiar pronoun *tu*. The deceased is present, she is made present. The intimacy of the relationship is created ("I am speaking to you as 'tu', excuse me, but he is the one speaking"); the transition to familiarity is a process that amplifies presence ("I gave you a hard time, I know," "you have to take care of yourself"), sometimes even intensified by the complete withdrawal of the clairvoyant: "He says you know what he means." The end of the message, most often, goes the opposite way and returns to the indirect style: "He tells me he kisses you, and that he will come back soon." The medium carefully prepares for separation. She does it grammatically, returning to the formal pronoun [*vous*], and to "he says that," slowly detaching the links she has just woven, blurring the presence, and lets the dead return to their place, among the dead, and the living to theirs, among the living. Except in one case I remember. A bereaved woman asks Michèle, at the end of the conversation, "Tell her I love her," to which she replies, "Tell her yourself." What each of these moments does is make the dead present, of course, but more importantly, doing so builds the experience of presence. For the spiritualist movement, it is a central therapeutic tactic.

Certainly, its therapeutic dimensions are numerous and all contribute to the effectiveness of what happens in a séance. There is an identifiable social support base, the fact that the collective of the living is, at least in the time of the meeting, present and warm, attentive and interested. The support provided by the dead is not to be overlooked, however. Especially not. Tanya Luhrmann, in a very nice article evoking the therapeutic value of prayer, questions the privilege granted to this theory of social support. This theory aims to explain that people who frequent places of worship are often in better health.[14] Of course, this support counts. But, she says, there is an important dimension that is hidden from the experience of these people: the fact that God himself appears to be helping them. It is not a question of pretending to resolve the question of the existence of the one helping, but of taking seriously the experiences that construct and pass through those who pray. People who learn to pray cultivate an ability to build relationships that have effects. This ability is itself based on the culture of experience, which Luhrmann calls *imaginal* experience. These experiences require imagination but are not necessarily imaginary. The imaginal experience is the experience that turns what is, or what must be imagined (God among the Christians studied by Luhrmann, the dead in the spiritualist movement), into a more real and better being. It is more real in the sense that it should no longer be taken as coming from inside the head, but must be felt as real and external. It is better in the sense that its intervention is intended to be benevolent, and it turns out to be so. This is what the spiritualist device mobilizes. It does not seek to arouse beliefs; it seeks to create experiences. And invites those who come to the séances to commit to it, according to their own modality. Spiritualists call this creative thinking. To feel the presence of the dead, Michèle says, you have to start by thinking about them and talking to them. Act as if they are there, and they could be there. Creative thinking aligns with this form of cultivation that is imaginal power. Like Luhrmann, she claims that summoning requires techniques, at the very least being available and alert to the possibility of feeling this presence and attesting to the success of the summons. Artifice and authenticity of the experience are no longer contradictory modes. On the contrary, the better the artifice is cultivated, the more the experience will be lived as authentic.

Another element must be pointed out in the case of the widower that I mentioned, the appearance of the grandfather. He is a therapeutic ally. And at the same time, he is part of a technical procedure. Reattaching the living to the world of the living should not be done too quickly. A benevolent deceased, often who died sometime ago, comes to play the role of intermediary in this reintegration. The spiritualist movement takes care to let time do its work.

A young woman had just lost her partner in an accident. They were about to be married. Hoping to renew contact, she went to consult a medium. This medium, probably inexperienced, and not taking into account the recent date of death, tells her that her fiancé wanted her to find someone else. This was terrible news for her. If he wanted her to do this so quickly, it was because their relationship meant nothing to him. The medium apparatus is designed to slow the pace. Except in rare cases, the dead cannot communicate immediately. They must first extricate themselves. It can take months, sometimes years. Other dead people then come to bring the message (we will see it in the next séance, when the clairvoyant says, "I am being given someone who was very optimistic"), testifying at the same time that someone is taking care of a dead person who is still not able to move, "held back" as they say. And that is what happens. Spiritualists know, in their own way, that the dead must find their place and that this requires work that is not that of mourning. For the dead, as for the living, the dead must become dead, that is to say, beings who are in their place and who have rediscovered the vitality of the dead—spirits, in short, from the spiritualist perspective. And this latency period has the effect of putting to work those who remain. They can help them.

At a séance on Thursday, January 13, 2011, this message is given to Jules, a young man in his twenties, who came with the photo of his friend Koj, who had died two years ago:

"This is not easy for me, I have an overpowering feeling of suffocation. This person is not very well either [the clairvoyant alludes to the fact that the previous person called had committed suicide], I feel an oppression, he does not give details. I am being given someone who was very optimistic, a bit naive, but gradually something happened, one disillusionment after another. There was nothing interesting or beautiful left. Already during his lifetime he was a loner. Do you remember him when he was still OK? [Jules says yes.] If you think of him when he was still well, it might help him get free. It is like he is in an enclosed cocoon, other entities are informing me. He was someone very kind, hypersensitive. He expected the world to be like him. These are real disappointments that came gradually. It's not even guilt, he's not there yet. When you think of him, you think of the end, and that freezes him even more. It requires an active approach on your part to see him happy and smiling. It is necessary and useful to send him positive thoughts and to visualize him happy and joyful. If you were urged to bring his photo, that is because there is something that can be done for him. You will have to come back in a while with his photo."

We have just witnessed another technical procedure. I knew the two young people and I knew through Jules that Koj had been a happy young man, full of life and plans, and that things had deteriorated in the past months. The world, he said, was off-kilter. So he left his parents a message at the start of a trip he ended a few days later, on the platform of the Blanche station in Paris: "I'm going to find the truth and I'm coming back." The description of the clairvoyant is correct, or rather it is *just* right. Because the question is not whether he is telling the truth or not; the question is to understand what his proposition affects, and its effects. It makes sense, it becomes true, it reconstructs history in a way that it now "holds." What could not be done can still be done. This proposal puts the bereaved young man in another position with regard to the defunct, above all, it transforms the regime of action and affects, in the same movement; it takes him from a passive situation to one of activity, and of sad passions to joyful passions. The living being, thus activated and touched, leaves with a responsibility: to reconstruct the past, actively, to open up other possibilities in the future. Act and transform ways of being, not retrospectively, but retroactively.

Fabricating, actively, to convey and feel possible pasts that have gone unnoticed or that have remained muted. It is the art of metamorphosis.

* * *

Friday, December 3, 2010, when the séance was about to end, there was
the appearance of an unsummoned dead person. Michèle announces it
by addressing a very young woman, sitting alone in the front row who,
apparently, came without a photo: "There is someone for you, coming
to see you. You don't know him. He's a young man, he's seventeen. He
just died. His name is Paul. It's a motorcycle accident. He does not yet
really know that he is dead. And his parents cannot help him, they are too
horror-struck, they cannot pray for him. I don't know why it was to you
that he has been sent. You will pray for him. He needs your help." And
right then, the young woman said, very emotionally, "This happened in
my family, a motorcycle accident, a young person also." The clairvoyant
replies, "So, no doubt that was why you were addressed." Having come
without a request, she leaves with a mission.

I find a relatively similar situation in the last séance I attended, on
December 7, 2014. Michèle has finished the work with the photos, then she
calls out to an elderly man, sitting alone in the rows of chairs. "Were you
in primary school in the countryside? I see a country school." He answers
in the affirmative. "Did you know a certain Roger? He is here. I see him
as a little taller than you." The gentleman says, yes, there was a Roger in
a class above his own. Michèle asks him to think of him; he's been dead
for some time and needs help, probably has no one to take care of him.
Then she immediately goes on to another story that justifies the fact that
the gentleman was called upon. She explains that the husband of a lady
who attended the séances was deeply alcoholic. After his death, however,
he seems to have decided to devote himself to people suffering from the
same addiction. So he spontaneously appears during a session in order
to ask a certain person, through Michèle, to pray for five young people
killed in a car accident blamed on alcohol. The parents, once again, were
too dismayed to allow their children to begin their progression—even to
realize their new state of death. In these stories joined up according to
the logic of the example, I find a characteristic of some of the stories that
populate the séances. They summon up others. They play a role similar
to narrative matrices, soliciting other narratives that make the stories
branch off. This is what Michèle does, beyond the apparent pedagogical
virtue of the precedent she invokes: Roger "calls" the alcoholic husband

who "calls" the five young men—dead people who have nothing to do with each other thus find themselves caught up in a narrative network, in which living people, in principle not concerned, are themselves mobilized. These stories amplify what the movement creates by soliciting the person who comes without a specific request. They register them in a network of relationships and commitments. They connect the person in an imaginary mode to others, living and dead, who solicit him or who have themselves been solicited. It wouldn't surprise me that this type of experience happens more often with very lonely people.

Signs are, of course, one of the resources. However, they do not often emerge during the séance, at least explicitly. They are part of the clairvoyant's toolbox. She has learned to read and connect them; to guess, from images, sounds or sensations, what will make up the content of the message. Michèle says these are "reminders." What she means by this term is unclear. The first thought is that the reminder marks a repetition or an emphasis, itself a crucial dimension of signs. But signs also "remind" in the sense that they reevoke things of the past and bring them to the present, in the form of memories incorporated with experiences lived by those who are with us no longer. The signs then take the form of physical sensations or perceptions. They cause a sensation, this time literally. They then perform presentification, both in the sense of moving the past into the present and of making a presence. Michèle says she feels oppressed, or feels a precise pain in a particular spot. So, if this feeling of being oppressed actually designates what the dead person is feeling *now* and so, in this case, does not play the role of bringing the past into the present, then other bodily manifestations will recall what he experienced, which adds to the consistency of the presence: Michèle sometimes has a feeling of suffocation or feels a sudden sore throat ("your father smoked a lot, didn't he?") and, on one disturbing occasion, a pain in the eye: "You have a pain in the eye, Madame? No? So maybe it was him. Really bad pain. The left eye." The parents of the young deceased remain silent. That was how the disease started.

When we met, Michèle didn't speak to us of this kind of reading of signs that guides the séances, but she did tell us about the signs that led her to clairvoyance, and in particular a prophetic dream whose astonishing accuracy led her to translate it as one of the commands she received to cultivate her gift.

In advanced pregnancy, she had a strange dream. She is in bed with her sister in her childhood home. In her dream, she wakes up, and looks out the window. Among the clouds, she sees baby limbs floating in the sky. She reaches out, grabs them, and begins to put the child back together. The baby is taking shape. But when she is about to complete the recomposition, a forearm and hand are still missing. At that moment, behind a cloud she sees the hand of Jesus appearing in the sky, catching the limb and carrying it away. The baby remains there without his arm. A few weeks later, Michèle gives birth, three weeks late. She says to us, you know when the children feel that there is something, they do not want to be born. It is often the case with these late births. The nurses are cradling the baby, talking to each other. Something is wrong. They are hesitating before showing her the child. Finally she finds out he is missing exactly that part of his arm and hand. They explain to her that it was an amputation. In the first few weeks of fetal growth, the limb was injured by a fibrous matrix and then healed.

This story led to others, all of which attested to the remarkable intelligence of this wise medium. One day the child became frustrated and desperate because he couldn't do something. She said to him, you are strong. It was Jesus himself who took your arm from you and offered you this magic hand, because he loves you. The child lived with this magic hand. She called it his "little arm and the magic hand" and, she said, he felt strong.

So that's the way Michèle was taught by her dream. She learned to give the power of blessings to oracles, things that reach us as a "to be lived."

Her son is a clairvoyant today and takes part in the Thursday séances. When he takes a photo from the envelope, he rubs it for a few moments against the scar left by the missing arm. "Ghost limb," Jules said after the séance, William James would have liked that.[15] Fabulation is not fictionalization. It is about extracting material from dreams to nourish reality.

Other signs are sometimes mobilized in the séances, but they are barely recognizable as such. They present themselves in the simplest, least elaborate mode, like images in realistic dreams that do not take off from reality: "You have never traveled." (The lady nods.) "It's amazing, I see a trip, I see you getting off a bus. You have never allowed yourself to travel. You devoted yourself to others; always for others. Would you like to take a trip? [Yes.] You are going on a journey. You have to do it. And I see you will have other relationships." The other medium intervenes: "I see the trip too, it is in Egypt I think, I saw pyramids." The sign here works in a way to give density to what might be lacking reality (a very vague statement, a prediction that looks more like an injunction than an announcement). This is the density it needs to be realized as it is, that is, *to have a reality effect*. This sign does not connect; it doesn't even symbolize. That is not its role. Its role is to detail (as in, adding details to give life to a story, to populate it with reality); effective details, that perform, or "actualize." The sign here is in the service of the prophecy. It is not its role to intrigue.

And when it is explicitly mentioned during a séance, the sign is named as such. It takes the form of an injunction, rather an induction, and receives no content. It is up to the people to seek that out. Has the person noticed the presence yet? Have there been any signs? The clairvoyant asks them to be on the alert. To make themselves available, to look for them. To create the favorable conditions to see or hear them, or even to learn to trust their own capacities to feel presences. "He tells me that sometimes he is near you, when you are at home, I see a desk, and he tells me that you feel that he is there, but that you are not sure of it." Michèle clearly takes on her role of sustaining existences and stimulating experimentation. Take a seat at a desk, take a walk in the woods, or turn on the radio without sound: those who remain are put to work. They acquire arts of noticing; they are initiated in the ethology of those who are no more, and to ways of welcoming them. They leave with invitations to respond to, biographies to update, stories to nourish. Stories to extend and accomplish.

My grandfather was about to be eight when his father died. I did not know this grandfather; my father was an orphan long before I was born.

Did he get this story from him? Was it his countless aunts and uncles whose happy memories he had of family occasions and the most fanciful card games? All these orphans, separated by haphazard fostering with family members who wanted them, had kept strong bonds, happy, meeting all the time, playing cards together every week, squabbling constantly, oh, said my father, how they could squabble! Laughing, teasing, playing tricks, sometimes arguing more harshly. What an astonishing contrast between how my father described these grown children, his father, his aunts and uncles, Arnold, Germaine, Cécile, Marthe, Mariette, Andrée, Gabrielle, Félix, Berthe, Suzanne, Raymond, Ghislaine, adults who retained childish joy, in life and in humor, and those who had abandoned them, whom my father told me had died of grief—that late train staying at the platform, the terrible advice from the father to his son.

Parents who died of grief; the joy that their children cultivated. Maybe that too was a fabulation. That's probably the regime they let themselves be guided by, a regime that leaves history open, a regime that leaves history alive, a regime that makes things start again.

8
PROTECTING VOICES

Our special brand of stupidity is the fact that we have made an "either . . . or" logic prevail, as if that were obvious, asking that what exists should exist "by itself" independently of us, or that it can be judged and reduced simply to human production.

—Isabelle Stengers, *La Vierge et le neutrino*

"Forgive me, Uncle, but do you really believe that Lotus Flower is real?"
"Nephew, if she isn't, why are you asking me about her?"

—Heonik Kwon, *Ghosts of War*

My friend Pauline Bastin told me that her mother, a few months after the death of her father, announced to her: "Your father came during the night."

Pauline asked her where he was, and her mother said, "He was outside the door."

Pauline asked her another question: "What did he do?"

Her mother replied, "He came and he looked to see if things were okay and then he left."

"So," continues Pauline, "I asked her, 'But you were dreaming?' My mother said, 'No, I wasn't dreaming, he came, I saw him. He came to see if things were okay. I wasn't dreaming, I dreamed *it*.' " Pauline was surprised at the language her mother had used because, she said, it was unusual for this woman of limited expression to do this work of elaboration and nuance, which she had never heard before. Her mother, she says, had tried to translate an in-between; she had to invent a formula to express something that is neither in the realm of dreams, nor in everyday reality, nor of sight nor the absence of what is perceived. With this enigmatic formula, says Pauline again, with this "I wasn't dreaming, I dreamed *it*," her mother invents new meanings for words. She creates homonyms; she diverts meanings. The verb "to dream" receives another meaning at the turn of the sentence by the simplest and yet the most sophisticated process, adding one simple auxiliary verb, the verb to have [*je l'ai rêvé*] and a pronoun that, in the context, becomes indeterminate: it [*l'*]. Pauline's mother enriches the language in order to share this experience with her daughter, communicating the right tone, distributing modes of presence and regimes of existence with this artful weighting. This is ontological tact. On the part of both mother and daughter, because this experience could only be the object of this desire to share and this effort of inventiveness, because Pauline explored a way of interrogating her mother that I would like to call "just." She does not ask what *her mother saw,* but what *her father did.* This changes everything because this question opens the story up. She addresses the situation exactly where her mother located her experience, in the milieu. She would probably have started off in a much more restrictive manner if she had formulated this question, from the start, in a subjective way: "What did you see?" The dead have so little leeway in their ways of being, such constrained action possibilities, that it is sometimes better to deliberately grant them the privilege of taking initiatives. The art of asking questions is called "erotetics." It is the art, as the etymology makes clear, of transmitting the desire to know, of engendering stories. The art of eroticizing versions.

Gillian Bennett, the English folklorist, cultivates this art with care. She has made it her vocation. She collects stories that allow her to draw "the map of interactions between the celestial and terrestrial worlds."[1] She does this in banal, everyday life. She questions women and men about how they create their interactions with their deceased and she does this on very specific grounds. She understands that investigations in which people are asked their opinion on life after death, on ghosts or the presence of the dead, at best result only in polite refusals, at worst in general theories of no great interest. How, then should one conduct research that does not take the form of these investigative procedures heavily marked by protocol, and in which people are asked to answer questions that obviously do not interest them or, in most cases, arouse their suspicion? Bennett's father has a podiatric practice in the suburbs of Manchester. Each consultation lasts for almost half an hour and does not demand attention from the patient as to what the doctor is doing. With her father's permission, she settled in the office, five mornings a week, and started talking to people during their consultations. She presented herself as someone with an interest in their experiences of relationships with the deceased. She maps the interactions between the celestial and terrestrial worlds in a place that takes care of what connects us most to the earth and makes us travel across it, by generating fabrications of travel stories between the two worlds. She keeps faith with her practice. She looks for connections and watches, with meticulous care, to give them every chance of being interesting.[2]

According to Bennett, the dead do not return, for the simple reason that they never left. Those who view this so-called return with concern, she says, are betting on a somewhat simplistic assumption that people would naturally have accepted to go along with the rationalization process. Obviously, if they are asked whether they believe in ghosts, people thus solicited will agree with those who, in the way in which they formulated their question, prompt the expected rational answers. So, Gillian Bennett no longer questions; she collects stories. About a deceased person, she might ask, "Do you still feel that he is near you? Do you still feel his presence?" Or, "You know we hear people say that their dead mothers or spouses come to see them from time to time. What do you do make of that? Do you think there could be something in it?" Stories start to flow, from a great number of them. Bennett further notes that if she questions these people about astrology, prophetic dreams and the presence of the deceased, the stories are not the same. The first, about astrology, are thin, told without details, a bit hasty, and often lead to stereotypical generalizations; the second are richer, connect a lot of other things, events and stories. These stories reflect the fact that the dead make storytellers of the living. But, even more interestingly, these stories all have a peculiarity: they are constructed so as not to privilege one version over another. The two possibilities, that of thinking the dead person has "really" returned and that of considering that it is a dream, or an impression, coexist, and their coexistence is conducted with remarkable care.

Before reading Bennett, I had come to the same observation, listening to the stories people shared with me during my meetings. This shows the strength and the intelligence of these stories.

So, for example, what Vanessa tells Gillian Bennett is similar, although in a different way, to what Pauline reported to me: "I *saw*," said Vanessa, stressing the verb, "my mother a few times, occasionally. But as to whether on these occasions it was in my head or if it was something else . . . It was night; did I dream of her? I do not know. But I saw her clearly. It happened once; but as to whether she was in my head or not, I don't know, and I can't remember if I was a little depressed. . . . But it occurred to me that it was some kind of warning that I was going to meet her, or something like that."[3]

In this story, we hear all the hesitations; a real narrative plurality is suggested. Is it in the head? Was it something else? Was I depressed? Did she want to let me know something? How can we dream and see clearly?

The experience of presence is not limited to that of the presence perceived, it can be experienced by another person, the narrator becomes the witness, but a witness that nevertheless goes through this experience and in which she finds herself engaged. Andrée says that her mother, at the end of life, suffered terribly. She says she turned inwardly toward her father, himself deceased, to ask him, "Look, enough is enough, you come looking for her, I can no longer see her suffer like that. . . . It was the 15th. On the 16th, at 2 a.m., the rest home called on the phone, Mom had died. As I wake up properly, I say to myself: 'That can't be right,' because when I said that to Dad, I didn't expect him to do . . . huh, like that . . . and now this! I asked myself if it was a bond to Mom that made that . . . because sometimes people also say, the bond to the mother . . . that she is let go and that."[4]

The way that Virgile—whose father committed suicide a few years ago—relates his experience to Laura Perichon presents the same structure, the same kind of oscillation, both when he reports on how automatic writing worked for him, allowing him to get in touch with him, and the evolution of their relationship over the years. "I'm going to say, at the beginning I consciously write and then, at some point, I have the impression that a kind of dialogue is established in the sense that I happened to ask a question and then *I*, or *something* flips in the answer. And I continue to write and then there, perhaps, a sort of dialogue or rather of expression settles down . . . I think for a good while I refused to let him go. And that as I work on past difficulties there is, I don't know for how long, a year maybe, I have the impression that well, he left, then, in peace . . . Finally, it might be eight or fifteen months, I don't know, in any case, I had this feeling that he was, that he is much less present, it has to be said. So is it 'present' in the sense that he takes up less space in me, or is it 'present,' more as a, in quotes, 'soul,' I don't know . . . Is this my perception or was he really present in one way or another? I mean, I don't know, anyway, there you go; yeah, I no longer have the impression because I associate the fact that he is less present with the fact that now he may be really gone and therefore more at peace."

This sensitive and actively maintained hesitation, this way of driving the story by making it waver around a point, certainly reflects the perplexity that the experience induces. But it not only translates it and it is not the only cause involved. First, this perplexity is actively aroused, unfolded, in and by the very fact of reporting on it. This perplexity is part of the investigation that the person produces from his experience; it is both the source and the product. And there is indeed an inquiry involved: they all search, explore, experiment with hypotheses, and each hypothesis stimulates another. This actively maintained hesitation, this constantly rekindled vacillation, at the same time constitutes the very stuff of experience: dream and perception communicate in a completely different way from usual modes, as with Pauline's mother or Vanessa; or, as with Virgile, what is self and what is "other" is redistributed, which is made particularly apparent when he says "*I*, or *something* flips in the answer" or when he imagines that, if I translate it in my terms, to be present is to be present to another, without it being possible to determine, in terms of causes, *what makes present*. We can just notice the acts, the techniques, the efforts, that bring about this "making present." This is what Virgile does, leading Laura to investigate with him these technical modalities that make up presence. But this actively maintained hesitation, these oscillations constructed in the statements, also attest to the person's effort to "pass" their experience, not only to transmit it but also to make it feel, to make it vibrate, to prolong it. *Protect* it. Because this is also what it is all about. These people protect their stories. But what are they actually protecting?

I have said that these stories are constructed in such a way that they do not allow the resolution of ambiguity. To say it like that, however, without some precaution, is risky.[5] Because we could always translate this proposition as the fact that people construct their statements in this way *in order to* protect themselves against the accusation of irrationality, by making concessions, the famous "I know very well, but still" noted by Jeanne Favret-Saada in the ambivalent speech of people confronted with witchcraft in the Bocage. It is true that some constructions could be similar to this "I know very well, but still." This is the case when one reads what Lettie tells Gillian Bennett, just before her mother died, a year after the death of her father: "I felt that whatever happened, Dad would come to meet her. Because she was sitting and she had that smile. Of course, *I know* they often sit like this just before they die. But she held out her arms, and she had that special smile that she had always had for him."[6]

This hypothesis, that people turn their words around in anticipation of the charge of irrationality, has taken two paths. The first is borrowed by folklorist David Hufford. He notes that people use a triple ambiguity register. On the one hand, first register, they make use of terms that support a complex of meanings that are both descriptive and interpretative; then, second register, they choose words that have several meanings; finally, third register, they use expressions that have both a metaphorical significance and a literal meaning. So very often people will use the expression "as if," which seems to prevent a literal interpretation: "It is as if she wanted to let me know something"; "It's like he's near me." According to Hufford, people would use these ambiguities to mask their speech. Besides, he adds, if we persist and make the respondents understand that we are not going to consider them crazy, the literal meaning emerges: it is no longer "as if"; it is, "he is near me" and "she wanted to let me know something." Consequently, the conclusion is obvious. People use this register of ambiguity precisely to protect themselves from this accusation.[7] If we allow that Hufford has a good sense that what he asks of his interviewees does not come out of nowhere, but from an extremely unhealthy milieu in which people know we think, if we were in their place, that it all comes down to their subjectivity, it still seems to me that his hypothesis of obtaining "more authentic speech" when he insists on it is not very convincing in the end. On the one hand, the fact that a testimony purified of contradictions may turn out to be more "true" than speech with contradictions, goes against what we learn from our daily experiences. On the other hand, thinking that "defensive" speech, in this case ambiguous speech, would be an artifact, does not allow us to assert that when the researcher insists on another kind of talk, he would obtain a more authentic testimony. What Hufford is experimenting with is the possibility of influencing the way people respond to him, by taking different postures. There is no rule that says one kind of speech deserves the stamp of authenticity more than another. The reassuring effect his insistence has on people does not reveal what their testimonies would "really" be; it just reveals that they might respond to what he is asking of them. He is attesting to the fact that the people he is interviewing pay attention to what interests him.

Gillian Bennett proposes another way to show why discourse is constantly wavering between rationality and irrationality. It is based on an observation that I myself noted at the beginning of this book. Our culture is characterized by the coexistence of contradictory versions. This coexistence is one element in the fabrication of stories.

Bennett's work is based on theories of narrativity that have shown that when a storyteller is narrating a legend, a dialectical relationship of affirmations and disputes is established between her and her audience that participates in the construction of the narration. According to these theories, legends make two normally distinct worlds communicate: the ordinary world and the world of the extraordinary or the supernatural. When the narrator is speaking, her audience will at times support her and at other times dispute her, or put what is being said to a test. The fabrication of a legend follows this process. Its successive versions will keep traces of the disputes that have polished its development. According to Bennett, this theory is relevant but incomplete, because the debate is not limited to the interaction between the narrator and her audience. It had already happened at an earlier stage. Each narrator sets up this debate internally. The dialectic is internal. Each time we tell a story, and more particularly a story that brings together phenomena considered to be out of the ordinary, we anticipate the challenge. As it is being told, the story then translates, and explicitly accounts for, these challenges that emerged in the internal dialogue. This gives us stories in which assertions (I would say that) are mixed with implicit moments of "but you could say that."

At a first reading, certain testimonies might confirm this interpretation. What Lettie said with her "I *know* they often sit like this just before they die" would be quite typical in this regard. But this "I *know*" could just as closely resemble the suggestion of Heidi, the midwife of the dead, that Lars's postmortem smile "could just as easily be a biological phenomenon that we have learned to recognize in the changes due to death." It could open. It would then be not an answer to a possible dispute but an invitation to create other versions.

What appears when we listen to these stories, and this is one of their crucial dimensions, is that they are rarely opposed dichotomously between the two very distinct regimes of rationality and the extraordinary; the events are not at the extremes of this polarization. On the contrary, the motive behind these stories, their driving force or their motive in the sense of what makes them move, is precisely the exploration of gaps, or making gaps communicate. Stories follow the movement of experience; that is what so aptly illustrates Virgile's "it flips." The narrative movement that flickers between versions—it's me, it's him—would be a repertoire of constant restarts. In other words, the "presences" of the dead show ways of being; they have ways of being present that are more complicated than that. They are not all or nothing, between "it was really there" and "it is a product of my subjectivity." I think, for example, of Rachid, who had lost his younger brother in a motorcycle accident and when asked, "Do you still feel his presence?," replied, "Yes, several times, through shadows, a noise, while dreaming. Also objects that belong to him. As soon as I feel his presence, first I accept this presence, and I try to leave doors and windows open, or even open the drapes to let the light in. I am not afraid of that kind of stuff, I stay pretty passive and try to roll with it. *When I feel his presence, I even open the window so he can go out if he wants.*"[8]

Dancer and choreographer Luc Petton told me about two encounters in the form of "presence." I am going to relate them in turn, focusing more on the second to try to make sense of what is so special about these stories. The first takes place with a deceased dancer, Jean-Michel. About thirty days after his death—I was there, Luc said, paying attention, because the number of days corresponded to those the Tibetan Book of the Dead indicates—five dancers gathered for a play that Jean-Michel had never danced and in a theater that he did not know. All had known the deceased, but each separately—except Luc and his wife, Marilén.

When they met up after the show in the dressing rooms and were chatting about how it went, they realized that everyone had felt the presence of Jean-Michel. Lara felt him dance next to her; Marilén felt him breathing by her side; another, who was at the other end of the stage, said he thought of him at one point. As for Luc, it was when he exited and went backstage that he felt his presence, specifying "his reassuring presence." Because of the choreography, they can pinpoint the moment exactly. It was the same for all of them. And there was no outside clue, says Luc, that could have made us think of him. How are we to understand this synchronization? Nothing explains it, and anyway the choreographer doesn't try to explain it. Instead, he makes it a technical issue; what interests him are the conditions that make this possible: "It's a thing where you are in the show, caught up in caring how it is going, and you are less concerned about yourself, you become an instrument, we are in the service of the performance. We are not *just* ourselves in these moments, we are traversed by it. The performance time, with its in-betweens and empty spaces, makes you able to be possessed by your role, you are no longer connected to the everyday real."

The second meeting was with one of Luc Petton's aunts of whom he was very fond. "One day, I go to my room, next to the kitchen. As I enter, I perceive her presence, at peace, soothing, as if she were sending a message of calm. And there, in that moment, I'm in a sensation, I don't doubt for a moment the veracity of my sensation, of my perception, the feeling *of the presence of the presence.* It is only two or three days after my mother told me of her death, but I think when it happened, she was dead." Petton speaks of *"the presence of the presence,"* something I have already heard in other accounts and whose redundancy here emphasizes both the particular level of the reality of experience and the necessity of registering it in a particular ontological configuration—that of the coexistence of two different ontologies. It is a presence that requires another, that requires the fact that someone is welcoming, whether he is just being, or offering himself as, "present." This particular configuration is reinforced by the coexistence of two modes of apprehension—Petton offers two terms, sensation and perception, joined together. We are already in the interstices, in an exploring movement inside the gaps.

In no way do these modes of presence obey the dialectic. Admittedly, these stories are doing ontological acrobatics, but never with huge leaps.

It is more of a dance, all the more so in that it does not happen by itself; inflections, vacillations, flips, restarts, set in motion by terms that are close and yet different, joined—sensations/perceptions, soothed/soothing, presence of presence. Friction, insistence, and repetition: these are their steps, their choreography.

The "as if" keeps coming up in this type of story. It is one thing that enables me to resume these stories. Note that there are multiple ways to understand it. This multiplicity attests to the fact that this trope has been the subject of a remarkable number of uses by the narrator himself and within the story itself, although it has only been used once. To put it more simply, the use of "as if"—like many other narrative techniques in this type of story—not only means several things but also *does* several things. These are active terms; they do things and they activate things.

The "as if" first refers to the one who "becomes present." Remember Andrée in chapter 6 who saw a sign of the presence of her father when the glasses exploded? She said, "It is as if he were injecting a bit of fun into something heavy and difficult," or Nanou, about thinking of a winning raffle ticket as equal to a gift of earrings: As if he wanted to give her a present. What is it about as if? It is not, in fact, about presence but about the content of the intention. It points, in the case of Andrée, to a reason that is not immediately legible, that it has to elucidate: the "as if" introduces a hypothesis for the good reason that someone may have to break the glasses in the hands of funeral guests. Similarly, in Luc's account, the "*as if* she were sending me a message of calm" is not about presence, which has a complicated degree of intensification and is adjusted by other means (the presence of the presence or, just as remarkable "I don't doubt for a moment the veracity of my sensation") but is about the possibility of intentions being in doubt. Something we never cease doubting, and not just with the dead.

Just as presence is attuned with sensation through the special reception it is given, the intentions of those who manifest themselves through this presence are shaped in the response offered—I am calmed, people laugh as the glasses explode, I give thanks for the gift. The possibility of receiving is a condition of the gift. In the case of Nanou and Andrée, it also linked with the sign, recognizable in its insistence: the glass will break twice, on similar occasions; the price of the raffle ticket is the same as that of the earrings, in a time and place marked by repetition.

Signs make signs: what do we do with this? Well, we do "as if." That is, we respond, we welcome it as an intention. This is what the sign asks. It operates on a background of misunderstandings. The answer gives the sign its meaning. It's pragmatic. If it's "like that," then you have to answer. What we are responding to becomes a sign. The "as if" is one of the paths the sign takes to become an enigma. "What do we do with this?" The story begins there.

Now we can see that expression is part of a game, of the mimetic arts, of playful fakery.[9] We carry on as if we can perceive or understand this as a message. Through this pretense, we make it possible for something to become what the "as if" was offering as a becoming. In such experiences, the "as if" designates the availability of the person to whom the sign is addressed, it puts them on the alert, it is a bait for meanings. We *ready ourselves* for something to happen. It is, moreover, this availability that Luc highlights in the first story, the fact of being "less concerned about yourself" that authorizes the dancer to allow the presence to be felt. But there, the "as if" is not necessary, the arrangement of spectacle and dance creates the conditions which will favor the experience.[10] This awakening of availability that "as if" translates, turns out to be very close to what Tanya Luhrmann was seeing in people who learn to feel the presence of God. Maintaining a conversation with God and being able to follow it in one's own thoughts require, according to her, a culture of true expertise: that of learning to pretend, to act "as if" God were really there, as if the voice that one hears inside were His voice. The "as if" of Christian evangelists allows them to actively make a presence exist. It implements and tests, in a pragmatic and active way, the porosity of the mind. At the same time it ensures the conditions for the exercise of a practice of discernment since its use involves keeping open the question of attribution when God manifests in thought. The analogy of these practices is, of course, only very partial, but, beyond all the differences, the point of similarity that constitutes the "as if" indicates one of its possible functions in these stories: it keeps the enigma open. It is its caretaker. The "as if" operates in the milieu, as it were; it holds the two hypotheses together by stamping the vacillation that links them. This would be one of the roles of the "as if," one particular mode of operation: to keep the vacillating space open and to protect the enigma.

So "as if" is a lever that opens possibilities. It doesn't step back to interpret. It doesn't take precautionary measures; it is a semantic device that makes it possible to affirm and actively maintain several possibilities: "it could be me; it may not be." The "as if" makes these possibilities hold and communicate. This means, since it assumes responsibility for connecting, that the "as if" takes account of the deviations and connects them by small approximations. This is also what the "as if" does; it approximates, in small steps.

"As if" operates in a similar manner, although not identical, to "presence of presence": it performs the coexistence of two ontologies; it explores the passage between two worlds by crossing over, always with almost imperceptible steps, it links two possible paths, zigzagging from one to the other, two ways of venturing, without jumping, without great leaps, without huge gaps.

These hypotheses do not explain the uses of "as if." They try to account for what it does, what it makes-do [fait-faire], how it fabricates the experience and how he tries to make it feel when it extends in a story. How it takes steps while making vacillations. Luc Petton is a dancer and choreographer. It is not surprising that it was with him that "as if" became a figure of movement for me.

This is what Bennett's analysis seems to miss: the movement the story makes. Bennett's work is based on an unquestioned assumption: these stories have the function of describing something that happened. I know of few stories that meet this definition. Stories do things, and they make something happen. They create. They are sensitive and they are touching. They make things and worlds exist; they transform, but above all, they are experiences. To assume that stories describe events, as her analysis assumes, is to imagine people in the same posture as those who interrogate them and who describe and think from these descriptions. This, of course, is the researchers' job, just as their job is not to confuse map and the territory, their descriptions and what they describe, the stories they make and what they do with them. But here, there is no map; the story *is* the territory.

When dancers experience a presence, the story they build together also creates that presence; it prolongs it, and this experience, this presence, above all, will be further prolonged, reexperienced, rearoused when Luc tells it to me. And I myself become a relay of this presence and this experience. I don't tell it, I pass it on. The stories keep the presence present, the dead alive. The stories insist on relaying. They regenerate vacillations. They are performances.

The story a presence makes us make up after that does not relate the event; it is itself an event. We live this presence, we relive it, which also means we revive it. Telling this type of story belongs to the arts of experimentation. Those who write to discover or explore what they think, know that writing and thought are made of the same material. The stories and experiences of these people to whom a presence comes are in a similar relationship. The stories are not "after" the experience, they are fully part of it. They start with it, and they prolong its vacillations as they reactivate them. This is why I said earlier that the story is of the same fabric as the experience. It's the same canvas, folding and unfolding at the same rate.

Stories cultivate the art of prolonging the experience of presence. It is the art of rhythm and the passage between several worlds, the art of making felt several voices. Vacillating, walking in the milieu, a real milieu, not along a line, but along multiple lines.

The ambiguity of these stories is therefore not the motive in the sense of motivation, nor is it a camouflage; it is the motive in the sense that it is the fabric, the texture, the stuff, the material, the very process of what activates thought from the start. The "as if," the ambiguities, the semantic inventions, the homonyms, the double meanings, the enigma—all constitute the experience. They are experimenting with the possibility of prolonging the effects of these plural forms of intention and agency. They take hold "by the milieu" giving the story its form of efficiency: making something felt, that is, making it exist. These stories transform and let themselves be transformed by the experience of an instauring journey in which they are fully involved. They actively deploy all possibilities. And that's their way of being, their power, their strength. These are statements which act or, more precisely, they are stories which relay presences which affect and "make-do." Daniel Bensaïd wrote, "The dead appeal to the living to wake up the dead."[11] Here a story begins and persists. Through the milieu.

Because what gives these stories strength and style is not the "or" or the "either . . . or," it is the "or thens." These are the "and, and, and . . . ," the "and then, and then, and then, and then, and thens" of a "something makes me think." "And" and "or thens" that follow other "ands" and other "or thens" that enlist each other. This is undoubtedly what made me love these stories so much, and the effects of ontological tact they bring to bear. One version always calls up another with *as if, perhaps it was,* sensations, presence of presence . . . It is the incantatory power of the stories; they regenerate presences and on this basis call up other stories. This is the erotics of the versions, which constitutes their mode of being as versions. Not only because, as Roland Barthes reminded us with bodily eroticism, because, by allowing a little glimpse, appearances/disappearances are staged,[12] but, above all, because they always call up others, they are a desire for persistence, a desire for other stories, a desire for vitality, they are incantatory.

These stories do not enchant the world, as we often say, but resist its deanimation. They do not fight against absence but compose with presence. In their very forms, in the grand inventiveness of their forms. The stories of the dead are endless stories, deliberately endless, they can always be reopened, begun again. These are stories that welcome, that acknowledge that something calls for thought, which means hesitating and fabulating. Actively. Stories are experiments. They are the workshops where being is made.[13]

Of course, insisting, as I do, on stories, might suggest that the dead are only their products; that their mode of existence is confined there; that the story "workshops" are the only place of their becoming real. But, let's not forget, I have a particular fix offered to me, the one by which I choose to honor these experiences with a deceased. It is these narratives that are doing the insisting and it is through them that I get to know them, that I perceive the ripples of their movement, like circles in the water once the stone has disappeared. This is what a young English literature teacher, Emily Thew, reminded me of after she told me a story of an encounter and its signs just when I was finishing this book. Because if the narration matters, what follows from it does just as much. For my very last lines I am going to ask this "following up" to give me three small points that tell us the story is not over, that it opens up to something else: other variations, other unfinished business, other presences.

"My father and I always shared a love of music. We loved listening together. The last day I saw him was on my birthday. I left right after that, and I never saw him again. Each of my birthdays, since then, has become a sad moment. I had a gold chain that he had given me. On my last birthday, I wanted to wear it. And I realized that I couldn't find it anymore. I was ashamed, I was sad. I felt this loss as a betrayal. I was listening to the radio and suddenly I heard, by chance, oh no, it was not by chance, the song that we both loved. A song about New York that used to remind him of his trip there, that song that always made me think of him and his happiness. When I heard this song, I felt even worse at first that I had lost the chain. And then I said to myself, this song comes from him. He can't be angry about the lost chain, he was telling me it doesn't matter, he was telling me he wasn't in the chain. So, I listened to this song as a gift and I felt good, calm. So I went back to where I had already looked for it and where I hadn't found it. The chain was there." I asked Emily if she would allow me to use her name. She replied, yes of course. But more importantly, she added, more importantly, add my father's name: Chris Thew.

So this could be what my father was asking for and what his own father was asking for, and perhaps even his parents, Joseph and Bertha, and each of their children, Arnold, Germaine, Cécile, Marthe, Maritte, Andrée, Gabrielle, Félix, Berthe, Suzanne, Ghislaine, and some of their children. That would be the meaning of this story. Georges cannot be an ancestor; one cannot be an ancestor at fourteen. Certainly, some of the dead continue to grow and age, I know some of them, provided that the living remember their birthdays and give them the opportunity to continue their lives. In another way, but always according to the cycle of time. You can say to some dead people, and I have often heard it, *today you would have been twenty years old, today you would have been thirty years old,* or maybe even, *today you are twenty years old,* and then *thirty,* because life goes on.

I don't think anyone was able to do it for Georges. And his life probably stopped a second time when his parents died. Then he had to stop aging because no one was looking after him. He was going to be forgotten.

I believe they knew, or understood, or felt, who knows?, that Georges would not find his place because no one was going to be there to commemorate him, that is to say, to remember "with him," to fabricate a past for him that would get longer and longer. Georges was going to disappear from lives and memories. He was on the way to never having existed.

I believe my father took care of this, taking the baton from the one who relayed this story to him. And so did his cousin. And probably others too. To become an ancestor, to accomplish this, you need many memories, at least a beginning of an accomplishment. Even if it is the memory of another, a memory by proxy, a memory that is taken up and relayed.

Georges remained present in the grief of his parents, in that story that had them dying of grief. *Take the earlier train my son.* Georges is still fourteen, he has not grown up, but he is still there, four generations later if I count the dream of my son, his great-great-nephew, as still prolonging his existence. Four generations is a lot for a deceased person with so few personal resources to remain in the memory of the living.

So I don't know if Georges's parents died of grief and I have stopped asking that question. Today, I am extending this story. It is my turn for fabulation, because this sorrow, in turn, requires me.

I do not know if Georges expects this from us, if this desire for memory is actually shared. No doubt his parents would be happy, which is something. It was perhaps to acquit this desire that my grandfather took charge of this story and, after him, my father. And it is also to my father that I am responding today, at the end of this book that he will not be able to read.

What can we know about what keeps us alive?

ACKNOWLEDGMENTS

Thanks to all who shared their stories with me. Unfortunately, and fortunately, the list is too long to cite everyone. Thanks to all who gave me advice and sometimes held me to my promise of following it. Thanks to Thibault De Meyer, Jérémy Damian, Thierry Drumm, Laurence Bouquiaux, Jules-Vincent Lemaire, Isabelle Stengers, and Philippe Pignarre for their invaluable aid in reviewing the manuscript. Thanks to everyone who waited for this book. Thanks to those who are no longer with us, and who made me write it.

NOTES

TRANSLATOR'S NOTE

1 Bruno Latour, *An Inquiry into the Modes of Existence*, trans. C. Porter (Cambridge, Mass.: Harvard University Press, 2016), 41.

2 Gregory Flaxman, *Gilles Deleuze and the Fabulation of Philosophy* (Minneapolis: University of Minnesota Press, 2012).

3 Vinciane Despret, *What Would Animals Say If We Asked the Right Questions?*, trans. Brett Buchanan (Minneapolis: University of Minnesota Press, 2016), 169–76.

4 *Angelaki: Journal of the Theoretical Humanities* 20, no. 2 (2015), special issue, "Philosophical Ethology II—Vinciane Despret."

1. TAKING CARE OF THE DEAD

1 Alexandra Schwartzbrod, "Un père éperdu," *Libération*, September 24, 2008.

2 Elsewhere she has the father "protecting himself from psychic damage." On this subject, see Dominique Memmi discussing what is at stake when theories of grieving are turned into prescriptions for work, in *La revanche de la chair: Essai sur les nouveaux supports de l'identité* (Paris: Seuil, 2014).

3 Louis Vincent Thomas, one of the major French anthropologists writing on death, exemplifies this recourse to the symbolic. A thirty-two-page online article of his contains no fewer than thirty-three instances of "symbol" or "symbolic" ("La mort aujourd'hui: De l'esquive au discours convenu," www.religiologiques.uqam.ca). Elsewhere Philippe Descola suggests that Whites invented the symbolic in encounters with "others" in order not to go mad (personal communication).

4 Magali Molinié, *Soigner les morts pour guérir les vivants* (Paris: Découverte, 2006), 123.

5 Molinié, *Soigner les morts*, 124.

6 Jean Allouch, *Érotique du deuil au temps de la mort sèche* (Paris: EPEL,

1997). Allouch, who is a psychoanalyst, in speaking to his clinical colleagues, notes that it is high time they distance themselves from the incongruity involved in passing over the difference between their ideas and the questions tormenting their patients, "even assimilating them, in the name of a scholarly principle that sees only nothingness after death, to simple beliefs" (67).

7 Molinié adds that according to this theory, mourning has become "a long and painful intrapsychic activity of remembrance that leads the survivor to progressively disinvest their object of love until they become able to substitute it for another." So mourners have to "undergo a reality test," which means they have to accept that the dead no longer exist in any way at all, except as a memory; *Soigner les morts*, 44.

8 On this point, see our constant reference, Bruno Latour's excellent work, *Modes of Existence*, and also his *On the Modern Cult of the Factish Gods*, trans. H. MacLean and C. Porter (Durham, N.C.: Duke University Press, 2009).

9 This letter was published in the correspondence the actor collected after her first book was published: Anny Duperey, *Je vous écris* (Paris: Seuil, 1992), 244.

10 Étienne Souriau, *The Different Modes of Existence*, trans. E. Beranek and T. Howles (Minneapolis: University of Minnesota Press, 2016). I am mainly referring, in this analysis, to the preface Stengers and Latour wrote on him for this new edition, "The Sphinx of the Work" (11–94), as well as Bruno Latour, "Reflections on Etienne Souriau's Les différents modes d'existence," trans. S. Muecke, in Levi Bryant, Nick Srnicek, and Graham Harman, eds., *The Speculative Turn* (Melbourne: re.press, 2011), 304–33.

11 Lise Florenne, "Instauration," in *Vocabulaire d'esthétique* (Paris: Presses Universitaires de France, 1990), 892.

12 Latour, *Modes of Existence*, 160.

13 It could just as easily relate to ethological practices, if that is understood in the sense Gilles Deleuze gave it: ethology is the "practical study of ways of being, that is, the practical study of what people and animals *can do*, not what they are, in their essence, but what they are capable of, what they do, the powers they have at their disposal, the trials they can put up with"; *Spinoza: Practical Philosophy*, trans. R. Hurley (San Francisco: City Lights, 1988), 125–27, translation modified.

14 Isabelle Stengers, "Penser à partir du ravage écologique," in *De l'univers clos au monde infini,* ed. Émilie Hache (Bellevaux: Éditions Dehors, 2014), 154.

15 No doubt the question of temporality should not be abandoned as quickly as I have suggested. But it doesn't arise so much as a problem to be solved as something to be located in a range of possibilities. But it seems to be more stable. Yet it remains complex, because it is relative. That makes the temporality of the dead multitemporal: those who die young, for example, continue to age for some of their loved ones. On each of their subsequent birthdays they gain another year, something those who die old don't do. But this first idea can itself be contradicted, when "those who remain" are, at the moment of dying, younger than the deceased. For example, they can, at a certain point, say, "Now I have passed the age she reached," a sign that the dead remain fixed, in a way, at the age of their passing.

16 Email to the author, November 29, 2016. See also Gilles Deleuze and Claire Parnet, *Dialogues,* trans. Hugh Tomlinson and Barbara Habberjam (New York: Columbia University Press, 1987), 2: "We think too much in terms of history, whether personal or universal. Becomings belong to geography, they are orientations, directions, entries and exits."

17 These "displacements" to which the dead invite us are all the more in evidence to the extent that while obliging us to think about places, they lead us to question and to throw into doubt our own locations. I also find this perspective, which situates the deceased in relation to displacement (and with the fact that the dead "displace" us), in the clinical work of Jean-Marie Lemaire, who has initiated certain therapies that bring together professionals and migrants to explore the very practical question, "how many kilometers from here are your loved ones (or those close to you) buried?" Putting it like this, many things are opened up, from the very concrete relations of distance the different participants will bring up, between here and there, with that of preceding generations, with those who matter and are no longer here, at the same time as it inscribes displacement into the relations between the living and the dead . . .

18 Gabrielle Guy, personal email, July 20, 2014.

2. ALLOWING YOURSELF TO BE INSTRUCTED

1 Heonik Kwon, *Ghosts of War in Vietnam* (Cambridge: Cambridge University Press, 2008), 104. I note, and this reference will become clear with what follows, that it was Philippe Descola who in September 2008 advised me to read Kwon. I told him that I didn't have much interest in the death of "others" and that I was concerned with our own. He retorted that, in point of fact, that what confronted the people whom Kwon was studying was the presence of "our" ghosts, that is, the bodies of those left there after the war.

2 Kwon, *Ghosts of War*, 106.

3 On this point, Pierre Zaoui has written a very good chapter on the joy of those who live on after a death, in *La traversée des catastrophes* (Paris: Seuil, 2010). This is an idea that Mathieu Potte-Bonneville nicely qualified as "vitalism in heavy weather"; see "Vitalisme par gros temps," *Critique* 8–9, no. 783–84 (2012), 677–86.

4 I am referring here to the work of the contemporary artist Sophie Calle, who on several occasions has decided to leave it up to someone else to conduct her everyday life, whether the novelist Paul Auster, who agreed to write the account of her future trip to New York in the form of a series of constraints designed to beautify the city (gather a certain number of smiles, decorate a particular place and take it over). Or the clairvoyant Maud Kristen, whom Calle asked to predict her future with the idea, she said, to go to meet it with a question: "What does destiny hold for me?" Auster's experiment was published as *Gotham Handbook, New York: Mode d'emploi* (Arles: Actes Sud, 1998); the work with Maud Kristen was the subject of several exhibitions and resulted in three books: *Où et quand: Berck* (Arles: Actes Sud, 2008), *Où et quand: Lourdes* (Arles: Actes Sud, 2009), and *Où et quand: Nulle part* (Arles: Actes Sud, 2009). [See also Sophie Calle, with the participation of Paul Auster, *Double Game* (London: Violette Editions, 1999).—Trans.]

3. THE TIES THAT KEEP THE LIVING AND THE DEAD TOGETHER

1 Examples come from Ruth Richardson, *Death, Dissection, and the Destitute* (Chicago: University of Chicago Press, 2000), 4.

2 I am thinking in particular of Elisabeth Claverie's research on pilgrims, Jeanne Favret-Saada's on "unwitchers" [désorceleurs], Christine Bergé's on spiritualists, Jérémy Damian's on dancers, Jean-Marie Lemaire's on consultants [concertants], Bruno Latour's on factishes, Magali Molinié's on the fruitful dead, Tobie Nathan's on dreamers, Isabelle Stengers's on healers, Alexa Hagerty's on midwives of the dead, Tanya Luhrmann's on Christians who cultivate internal meanings, and Heonik Kwon's on ghosts, just to mention a few of those referred to, often too briefly, in this text.

3 Molinié, *Soigner les morts*, 137.

4 Molinié, "Faire les morts féconds," *Terrain* 62 (2014), 72.

5 Molinié, "Faire les morts féconds," 80.

6 Here Molinié is inspired by Bruno Latour's *Modes of Existence*, mentioned in chapter 1.

7 Christophe Pons, *Le spectre et le voyant: Les échanges entre morts et vivants en Islande* (Paris: Presses de l'université de Paris-Sorbonne, 2002), 167.

8 As demonstrated by William James in *Essays in Psychical Research* (Cambridge, Mass: Harvard University Press, 1986). One should add that in Iceland a bad medium doesn't throw the whole profession into doubt (any more than a bad doctor, among us, does not submit the whole field to accusations of charlatanism). One just has to be careful dealing with a bad medium.

9 Pons, *Le spectre et le voyant*, 38.

10 See Isabelle Stengers, *La Vierge et le neutrino* (Paris: Découverte), 2006.

11 Ian Hacking, *Rewriting the Soul: Multiple Personality and the Sciences of Memory* (Princeton, N.J.: Princeton University Press, 1995); *Mad Travelers: Reflections on the Reality of Transient Mental Illnesses* (Charlottesville: University Press of Virginia, 1998).

12 Suffrages are specific kinds of prayers (or pious acts taking the place of prayers) addressed to the saints or to God in order to help purify the deceased and to deliver them to the purifying fire. They can take several forms: prayer, priestly oblation, fasting, alms, or any other expiatory form. A penalty [peine] must be expiated by a penalty [peine].

13 Jean-Claude Schmitt, *Les revenants: Les vivants et les morts dans la société médiévale* (Paris: Gallimard, 1994).

14 Guillaume Cuchet, "Les morts utiles du Purgatoire, concept théologique, représentations et pratiques," *Terrain* 62 (2014), 97. I should add that, according to Jacques Le Goff, the idea of trips to the hereafter

and of the dead coming back, emerging from pagan and Celtic cultures, already existed in the popular literature, but had not yet found outlets in scholarly texts. See Le Goff, *La naissance du purgatoire* (Paris: Gallimard, 1981), 117. It was because the Church's mistrust of popular theories or theologies retreated to some extent between 1150 and 1250 that purgatory as a place could be born.

15 I might add, without wanting to open the debate, that, according to Le Goff, those who are called ghosts [*revenants*] are not favored in purgatory. Purgatory would channel them, if I can put it like that; they only come back for a specified time, by request, and are not given to wandering. Le Goff notes, for example, that in reluctant heretic villages in purgatory, souls continue to wander (393). And the term "ontological refugee" comes from Heonik Kwon's work, designating roaming ghosts in the postwar context in Vietnam; *Ghosts of War,* 16.

16 These two presentations were made during a workshop that brought us together at the end of January 2014 around the creation of a play, *Un jour,* by Massimo Furlan and Claire de Ribaupierre (compagnie Numéro 23/Prod.).

17 Schmitt, *Les revenants,* 19.

18 Schmitt, *Les revenants,* 13.

19 Tobie Nathan and François Dagognet, *La mort vue autrement* (Paris: Découverte, 1999), 101.

20 Schmitt, *Les revenants,* 18.

21 I say "post-Freudian" with the qualification that, according to Allouch (*Érotique du deuil*), the phrase "work of mourning" is only used once in Freud's *Mourning and Melancholia*; it can mostly be attributed to his followers.

22 Without bringing into account more recent factors, as thoroughly shown in Memmi's *La revanche de la chair,* professionals working with the dead have succeeded in revalorizing their practices that had been weakened as a result of the demise of rituals by encouraging mourners to take on a more engaged relationship with the dead in the form of a very "psychologized" grieving.

23 Emily Martin, *Bipolar Expeditions: Mania and Depression in American Culture* (Princeton, N.J.: Princeton University Press, 2007).

24 The *Diagnostic and Statistical Manual of Mental Disorders* describes the symptoms for each mental condition that psychiatrists have to learn to recognize in order to diagnose their patients. At the moment they use

DSM-V, which brought up quite a few controversies in its preparation. In brief, for our purposes, it suggests that any mourning that goes on longer than a few weeks could be diagnosed as a pathology.

25 Schmitt, *Les revenants*, 254.

26 Rudolf Bultmann et al., *Kerygma and Myth: A Theological Debate*, trans R. H. Fuller (London: SPCK, 1953), 3–5.

27 Tanya Luhrmann, "To Dream in Different Cultures," *New York Times*, May 14, 2014, A27. Thanks to Thibault De Meyer, who drew this article to my attention when he read the manuscript.

28 Jeanette Winterson, *Why Be Happy When You Could Be Normal?* (New York: Grove Press, 2011), 196. Thanks to Beatriz Preciado for suggesting this book as a contribution to this research.

29 Here I refer once again to the work of Bruno Latour, particularly his *Factish Gods*. Elisabeth Claverie also writes, "The social sciences are in large part constituted around a radical denunciation of religion as producing illusions, these same illusions being what the social science researcher should debunk as an invisible agent unknown to the actors, an agent who manipulates them without their knowledge in all sectors of social activity"; "La Vierge, le désordre, la critique," *Terrain* 14 (1990), 60–75.

30 Angel Yankov, "Les vampires *Drakous* de Dolène," in *Malmorts, revenants et vampires en Europe,* ed. Jocelyne Bonnet-Carbonell (Paris: L'Harmattan, 2005), 313.

31 This particular point was inspired by Claverie's pragmatic position taken up in her research on pilgrimages to the Virgin of Medjugorje. She doesn't try to explain how the apparitions take on meaning according to different economic, religious, or political context that produce them, but rather inverts the take by sticking to observing what the *apparition makes appear* in terms of political and economic conflicts. For instance, the appearance of dead without tombs, victims of the executioners of the Second World War; see Clavarie, "La Vierge en action," *Terrain* 44 (2005). "The first thing . . . the apparition did was make something speak that should be silenced, should be a secret, something that until now had not been said"; Clavarie, "Apparition de la Vierge et retour des 'disparus,' " *Terrain* 38 (2002), 41–54.

32 Jay Winter, *Sites of Memory, Sites of Mourning: The Great War in European Cultural History* (Cambridge: Cambridge University Press, 2014), 71.

33 Julian Holloway and James Kneale, "Locating Haunting: A Ghost Hunter's Guide," *Cultural Geographies* 15, no. 3 (2008), 297–312.

34 This inquiry was carried out by T. B. Posey and M. E. Losch, and referred to in an article by Dennis Klass, "A New Model of Grief from the English-speaking World," https://www.academia.edu/1625789/A_New_Model_of_Grief_from_the_English_Speaking_World.

35 "We are sure that the Virgin" [who appeared to the Medjugorje pilgrims], Isabelle Stengers writes, not without irony, "can be reduced to human subjectivity, the only question that remains is which of our human sciences will emerge as the most qualified to do the work"; *La Vierge et le neutrino,* 192. On the topic of the Virgin, see the wonderful book by Elisabeth Claverie, *Les guerres de la Vierge: Une anthropologie des apparitions* (Paris: Gallimard, 2003); for unwitchers, see also the classic study by Jeanne Favret-Saada, *Deadly Words: Witchcraft in the Bocage* (Cambridge: Cambridge University Press, 1980), and her excellent *Désorceler* (Paris: L'Olivier, 2009).

36 Christophe Pons, *Les liaisons surnaturelles: Une anthropologie du médiumnisme dans l'Islande contemporaine* (Paris: CNRS, 2011, 108).

37 This attempt at exorcism on the part of the human sciences also has a parallel, coming from these same sciences, in their denunciation of the "taboo on death" (the two are linked). So, writes the anthropologist Johannes Fabian, referring to Werner Fuchs, "It turns out that sociologists and psychologists who make 'suppression' of death the cardinal topic of their analyses . . . are in fact arguing very much like Christian theologians who lament modern man's apparent indifference to death. The suppression hypothesis, Fuchs argues, is an interpretation supported more by interests in preserving the vanishing influence of religious institutions than by empirical facts"; Johannes Fabian, "How Others Die: Reflection on the Anthropology of Death," *Social Research* 39, no. 3 (1972), 552. One has to wonder if the taste for the anthropology of death might not denote a kind of nostalgia invented by those who were missing the dead that they had eliminated.

38 As is the case with scientific research on animals, which is particularly instructive in this regard. See Despret, *What Would Animals Say If We Asked the Right Questions?*

39 Claverie, *Les guerres de la Vierge,* 353.

40 Following Isabelle Stengers, one can add that it is exactly the same type of false problem identified by Bergson. For example, asking "why

is there something rather than nothing" implies emptying the scene of everything that exists. Then one thinks of emptiness coming first, forgetting that first everything would have to be cleared out. Hence, from my point of view, the remarkable interest that the study of the Drakus holds, or, further from us, Plutarch's fascinating thoughts on the disappearance of the oracles. See Stengers, *La Vierge et le neutrino*, note 126; Plutarch, *Moralia*, vol. 5, *On the Obsolence of Oracles*, trans. F. C. Babbitt (Cambridge, Mass.: Harvard University Press, 1936). Also, the elegant analysis Katrin Solhdju gives Plutarch's text shows how it is useful for clinical work: *L'épreuve du savoir: Propositions pour une écologie diagnostique* (Paris: Dingdingdong, 2015).

41 [With the senses of "badly addressed/spoken about" and "badly treated."—Trans.]

42 Maurice Bloch, "La mort et la conception de la personne," *Terrain* 20 (1993): 7–20.

43 Emmanuel Carrère, *My Life as a Russian Novel: A Memoir*, trans. L. Coverdale (New York: Metropolitan, 2010), 62.

44 Eduardo Kohn, *How Forests Think: Toward an Anthropology beyond the Human* (Berkeley: University of California Press, 2013), 18.

45 In the Middle Ages, Molinié tells us, when people gave accounts of meeting a ghost, clerics had the habit of responding by answering five questions: "Who is coming back? When? Where? How? And why?" *Soigner les morts*, 189.

4. WATCHING OVER THE THINGS THAT MATTER

I owe it to Agnès Lejeune for suggesting Kundera's *The Book of Laughter and Forgetting*. The title of this chapter echoes the work of philosopher Didier Debaise, especially what he advances in the field of speculative philosophy, that it constitutes a site for cultivating important fluctuations. On this, see his interesting analysis of Whitehead in *Nature as Event: The Lure of the Possible*, trans. Michael Halewood (Durham, N.C.: Duke University Press, 2017). This "importance of importances" also owes a lot to the work of the GECO (Constructivist Study Group), which has often accompanied me in this research.

1 Arata Tendo, *L'homme qui pleurait les morts*, trans. Corinne Atlan (Paris: Seuil, 2014). One should not overlook the extent to which certain ideas in this novel approach Judith Butler's in *Frames of War*: "Grievability . . .

means that this is a life that can be regarded as a life. . . . Without grievability, there is no life, or, rather, there is something living that is other
than life. Instead, 'there is a life that will never have been lived,' sus-
tained by no regard, no testimony, and ungrieved when lost." *Frames
of War: When Is Life Grievable?* (London: Verso, 2009), 15.

2 Opting for this formulation, they want to "be remembered," rather
than "the dead want us to remember them," I chose to emphasize a
particular dimension of this story, the active and present will of the
dead. Saying that "the dead want us to remember them," on the one
hand, could too easily be shunted back to a past desire in an unequiv-
ocal way (emerging at the time they were alive, which the epigraph I
chose for this chapter could make one think), it is the present dimension that is emphasized with "they want to be remembered." On the
other hand, the active dimension seems to me better conveyed by
making the dead the subject of the verb, for which the living occupy
henceforth the grammatical function of the agent.

3 Patrick Williams, *Gypsy World: The Silence of the Living and the Voices
of the Dead* (Chicago: University of Chicago Press, 2003).

4 "What we have to do," said Deleuze, "is catch someone else 'telling
tales,' caught in the act of 'telling tales.' . . . These capacities of falsity
to produce truth, that's what mediators are about." Gilles Deleuze,
"Mediators," conversation with Antoine Dulaure and Claire Parnet,
in *Negotiations 1972–1990*, trans. M. Joughin (New York: Columbia
University Press, 1990), 125–26.

5 Donna Haraway, *When Species Meet* (Minneapolis: University of Minnesota Press, 2008), 162.

6 I am indebted to Maria Puig de la Bellacasa (during a terrific conversation on March 12, 2008) for this metaplasm that indicates the dead
regenerate, that is to say, among other possible significations, ask for
a "resumption."

7 Series created in 2001 by Alan Ball, after the death of his sister. This
advice came at the same time as another, that was given to me by two
journalists in succession, whom I had met in the course of my work
at the time, Serge Canasse (October 4, 2007), and Nathalie Massart
(January, 16, 2008), to go to see morticians. My son, Jules-Vincent
Lemaire, later facilitated this encounter by organizing an evening
devoted to the theme of the dead at the "À nous de voir" festival in
Oullins.

8 John Gray's 2005 series, suggested by Isabelle Stengers.

9 Directed in 2005 by Glenn Godon Cardon.

10 Created in 2007 by Graham Yost.

11 Created in September 2003 by Meredith Stiehm.

12 [From the Old French *malemort,* someone who had suffered a cruel and tragic death.—Trans.]

13 We are told that this sets up some very interesting technical problems to do with "resemblance," similar to that the people who build so-called AI portraits encounter. Too many elements in the reconstruction of the face, for example, too many precise details, can in fact hinder chances of recognition. Work is "through approximations" to allow others, those who should recognize them, to situate themselves in these proximate zones where recognition can take place.

14 On this point see Albert Piette, who suggests that the dead, in the case of their perseverance with us, are "re-present"; *Le temps du deuil: Essai d'anthropologie existentielle* (Paris: Éditions de l'Atelier, 2005). I should note that reading Piette also came out of advice during my learning trajectory given to me by one of his former doctoral students Catherine Remy, September 13, 2007. Catherine was an active networker: sometime later, Albert Piette wrote to me, most kindly sending me the books written on the basis of the death of his father.

15 Magali Molinié, "Pratiques du deuil, fabrique de vie," in *Faut-il faire son deuil?,* ed. Pascal Dreyer (Paris: Autrement, 2009), 24–35.

16 Conventional and inappropriate treatment if one is interested in the dead, rather than in death. The fact that ceremonies constitute a response to death and put communities in a situation where they have to reinterrogate and recreate their links, is another approach, incidentally much more interesting when it is done well. I am mostly thinking here of the works of Maurice Bloch and Rita Astuti; see "Are Ancestors Dead?," in *A Companion to the Anthropology of Religion,* ed. Janice Boddy and Michael Lambek (Hoboken, N.J.: Wiley-Blackwell, 2013), 103–17.

17 This recomposition can also take a literary turn, and not only when those left behind write for those who are no more (as do Patrick Chesnais or Albert Piette, but many others could be mentioned), but equally by delving into literature to find things that sometimes seem to have been written for them. This is a theme in Janet Frame's *Daughter Buffalo*: "In the midst of confusion of loss and grief and change of

status (my sister was raised from a laughing devil who could lie and cheat, torture with pinches and back thumps, to a heavenly angel who could have harmed no one), of departures without return, I took the path of escape already well-worn in my life—the path to the literary death" (London: Pandora, 1990), 63. My colleague Marc Delrez suggested this book in September 2008.

18 Roland Barthes, *Mourning Diary*, trans. R. Howard (New York: Hill and Wang, 2010), 190.

19 Martin Julier-Costes figures in my learning trajectory because I met him while following the advice his mother gave me during a seminar in Geneva, April 24, 2008. His doctoral thesis is "Socio-anthropologie des socialisations funéraires juvéniles et du vécu intime du deuil: Les jeunes face à la mort d'un(e) ami(e)" (University of Strasbourg, 2010).

20 Allouch, *Érotique du deuil*, 348.

21 Allouch, *Érotique du deuil*, 289.

22 [In French, theatrical "répétition" translates as "rehearsal."—Trans.]

23 On this, see Gilles Deleuze, suggesting that the first drink "repeats" the last; *Abécédaire*, "B, comme boisson." [Deleuze's *Abécédaire was* an eight-hour series of interviews between Gilles Deleuze and Claire Parnet on French television, later published as Claire Parnet and Gilles Deleuze, *Gilles Deleuze from A to Z* (Los Angeles: Semiotext(e), 2012).—Trans.]

24 Allouch, *Érotique du deuil*, 120. Via email, Jérémy Grosman put me on to a passage from Gilbert Simondon's *Imagination et invention*: "The symbolic function of imitation, when it is used in an intense way, has a close correlation to the revival of memory; it generates the mimed object and makes it live through evocation, as if the mimed object took possession of the mimer. During funerals in ancient Rome, the procession was preceded by performers who evoked the memory of the departed by reproducing his way of walking, his tics, everything that constituted the caricature of his movement and individual attitudes that inalienably belonged to this person. This miming activity had the same meaning as the portraits, statues, and *imagines* of the ancestors. Even today, the evocation of the departed is accompanied by a certain effect whereby their habits are conveyed; the choices they have made, the words they would have used in one situation or another" (1965; Paris: Presses Universitaires de France, 2014), 92. A few minutes after this email come in, I had another from Fabian Miche, who wanted to bring the visual artwork of Moira Ricci to my attention. She

superimposes photos of herself on others of her mother. This is how she describes it: "After the death of my mother, I turned myself into images in such a way as to be close to her and look at her with dresses and hairstyles more or less in the style of when the photo was taken, in the simple, modest way that that she had the habit of dressing in." Go to http://www.strozzina.org/manipulatingreality/e_ricci.php to see the photographic works her mother "became" to keep her close to her.

25 Pierre Bergounioux, *La Toussaint* (Paris: Gallimard, 1994).

26 Bergounioux, *La Toussaint*, 69, 72.

27 Winterson, *Why Be Happy?*, 179.

28 I am picking up again on the critique in chapter 3 by Julian Holloway and James Kneale ("Locating Haunting") as well as that of Heonik Kwon in chapter 2 (*Ghosts of War in Vietnam*).

29 Tobie Nathan, *Nous ne sommes pas seuls au monde* (Paris: Découverte, 2002), 61.

30 In this pragmatic perspective, you can read Albert Piette's interesting analysis: "The human sciences, for the most part, have no interest in supernatural beings as present in a situation. They leave any interpretation of this type of situation up to theology, while they consider them to be passive backdrops, helping in the analysis of values, cultural representations of the group, or even individual psychologies"; *Le temps du deuil*, 119.

31 Emilie Cameron, "Indigenous Spectrality and the Politics of Postcolonial Ghost Stories," *Cultural Geographies* 15 (2008), 383–93.

32 Cameron, "Indigenous Spectrality," 389.

33 Kiyoshi Kurosawa, conference organized with the *Revenants* [Ghosts] exhibition at the Louvre, March 12, 2011.

34 The title was translated, surprisingly, as *L'aventure de Madame Muir*. It is hard to see the justification for effacing the ghost simply as an effect of style or translation. No doubt we francophones have more problems with ghosts than Anglo-Saxons do.

5. EXTENDING THE WORK

1 Siri Hustvedt, *The Sorrows of an American* (London: Sceptre, 2012). It was thanks to a suggestion (still on my learning curve) my friend Serge Gutwirth gave me on September 4, 2008, that I read this book.

See also in Albert Piette the idea of a contract passed in writing with the dead: "It is thus that I suddenly had the idea of a sort of contract, very implicit, between the life of my father, my experience of his death, and my ethnographic know-how that consisted in observing and describing facts and people's actions. The clauses of the contract remained undefined"; *Détails d'amour ou le lien par l'écriture* (Paris: L'Harmattan, 2003), 9.

2 Delphine Dori, "De l'art médiumnique à l'art brut, l'exemple d'Augustin Lesage," *MethIS* 4 (2011), 63–79.

3 Michel Thévoz, *Art brut, psychose et médiumnité* (Paris: La Différence, 1990), 142. Elsewhere he writes in the catalogue of the exhibition held in 2000 at the *Maison rouge*: "Was it necessary for the bourgeoisie's seizure of art to be fatal, for the pretension of a laborer to communicate with Leonardo da Vinci seem less meaningless than that of becoming a painter?" These rationalizations are not nearly as stupid and violent as others I have found elsewhere, and I will spare myself another bout of irritation by reporting them. Yet the most caricatural deserves a mention, just for fun. Lesage seems to have found, in this spiritual-pictorial adventure, the equivalent of a therapy about unconscious death anxieties, and probably a psychotic issue with no clinical history. It was worth a try: redefine the work as therapy justified by the creation of an unconscious reason and through a diagnosis of an illness almost certainly as much masked by the therapy as it remained latent!

4 Cited in Christine Bergé, *La voix des esprits: Ethnologie du spiritisme* (Paris: Métailié, 1990), 173.

5 The philosopher Thierry Drumm tells me that William James had experimented with modifications of consciousness in order to gather conditions that allow certain knowledges to have consistency. James writes in *The Principles of Psychology* (chapter 13) that he tends to suspect that the ultimate philosophy of difference and resemblance should be constructed out of intoxicating experiences, particularly nitrous oxide ("laughing gas") that allows for "intuitions whose subtlety is denied in the wakeful state"; *Principles of Psychology* (New York: Henry Holt, 1890), 531n.

6 In a very nice article dedicated to bringing together Sigmund Freud and William James on the status of the dead, Thierry Drumm picks up on the incident described by Freud in *The Psychopathology of Everyday*

Life, when he can no longer remember the name of the fresco painter in Orvieto cathedral, Luca Signorelli. Drumm invites us to look at the context in which this name, referring to a dead person, refuses to come out and remains stuck "on the tip of the tongue." This context in which an "active fault line" signals itself through this name refusing to come back but is still there, could encourage a kind of trance since the incident happened during a train trip. Making use of this context, Drumm builds a series of heterogeneous relations that he doesn't reduce to the same, but with which he tries to intensify the continuity: the train here becomes a "medium," that is, a mediation device, first because it generates daydreaming, a particular state of consciousness that "makes things felt" and then because it is not without evoking that which, at a certain moment, opens the way to theories of trauma. Drumm emphasizes that Freud made a contribution to moving the notion of trauma from the domain of physiology to that of psychology on the occasion of establishing issues, without physical etiology, among people who had been through a railway accident. Thierry Drumm, "Des rapports aux morts: Freud ou James?" (n.d.). Perhaps it is not fortuitous that Georges's story, the death that keeps coming up in my own journey, has some relation to this type of accident.

7   Dave Van Ronk and Elijah Wald, *The Mayor of MacDougal Street: A Memoir* (New York: Da Capo Press, 2008). This story was sent to me by Jérémy Damian, whom I want to warmly thank again, for this and all the other relevant help.

8   Letter to his brothers, 27 December 1817, in John Keats, *Letters*: "when man is capable of being in uncertainties, Mysteries, doubts, without any irritable reaching after fact & reason." I would also like to refer to Donna Haraway, since she made me aware of this question in *Staying with the Trouble: Making Kin in the Chthulucene* (Durham, N.C.: Duke University Press, 2016).

9   Bruno Latour, "Factures/Fractures: From the Concept of Network to the Concept of Attachment," trans. Monique Girard Stark, *RES: Anthropology and Aesthetics,* no. 36 (Autumn 1999), 20–31.

10 This dream came out of interviews conducted by my student Margaux Doutrelepont in the context of her final thesis in psychology, "Le rapport aux morts chez les personnes maghrébines à Bruxelles (Free University of Brussels, 2012).

11 Email, October 18, 2013. Marcos Mateos and I have been keeping up a

regular correspondence since the beginning of my inquiry. It would be an understatement to say that his help has been valuable. For each idea I propose to him, he opens unexpected approaches. He comes up with formulations that find a new angle on the problem, and translates each life event into food for thought. I remain his apprentice in this area I am exploring.

12   "Excluded from conscious life, the dead never stop visiting dreams, to the point one might think they have a particular appetite for this space: from the dream that follows the death, coming the next day or the following, to those people that have dreams, and not necessarily the immediate family, months or years after the death, in which the dead deliver their recommendations to the living. And this is perfectly understandable if we understand the usual dream modalities, that come to think the unthinkable, forge concepts of the invisible, fabricate a possible that wide-awake thought, stuck in the ruts of habitual thought, does not manage to imagine"; Tobie Nathan, *La nouvelle interprétation des rêves* (Paris: Odile Jacob, 2011), 206.

13   This is what François Ellenberger called, apropos of the act of remembrance, "the illusion of intention": "At every point actual consciousness appears to itself as the necessary and sufficient source for its mnestic participations, memories or images." *Le mystère de la mémoire* (Geneva: Éditions du Mont-Blanc, 1947), 11.

14   Email, January 11, 2012.

15   I recently had a letter from a woman, Félicianne Ledoyen. In 2002 she lost one of her friends, whose death left his young wife in despair. She herself was undergoing treatment for breast cancer and didn't feel she had the courage to care for her friend. Both of them went through a tough time. Two years later she is in her garden and he appears to her. He tells her: "She needs you." Thinking it was a hallucination, she doesn't reply. But sometime later, she has a dream. Her friend is there, dressed the same way as when he appeared the first time, and asks her to call his spouse. "She needs you." She phones. Yes, her friend was right. She really did need her. She concludes: "What did I see? A ghost? A hallucination? An apparition? I don't know, but I saw something. And as for my dream, that was certainly real."

16   Tobie Nathan suggests that the dead install a rigor at the heart of the living. As soon as a dead person appears in a dream, we can advance

the hypothesis that it might be about restoring order. And he says this is where one can recognize the work of a lawyer, who, in carrying out the will of the dead, "interrupts the chaos of absence"; Nathan, *La nouvelle interpretation*, 207. The philosopher Robert Harrison invokes the fact that the dead take care of future generations and their calls for order concern them. "The dead," he writes, "like to stay close to the living"; *The Dominion of the Dead* (Chicago: University of Chicago Press, 2003), 1. It is in response to this wish that we bury them close by, confiding them to the earth beneath our feet because one of the ways the dead accomplish themselves is through watching over those who remain to hold them to the task of caring for those who will follow. Harrison writes earlier in *Dominion*: "In the human realm the dead and the unborn are native allies, so much so that from their posthumous abode—wherever it be—the former hound the living with guilt, dread, and a sense of responsibility, obliging us, by whatever means necessary, to take the unborn into our care" (ix).

17 Pons, *Le spectre et le voyant*, 125.

18 On this, see Bruno Latour's work on the metamorphosis of religious beings in the *Inquiry into the Modes of Existence* and *Rejoicing, or The Torments of Religious Speech* (London: Polity, 2013).

19 Alfonsina Bellio, "Femmes qui vont avec les morts en Calabre," in Bonnet-Carbonell, *Malmorts, revenants et vampires en Europe*, 201–20.

20 Bellio, "Femmes qui vont," 218 n. 22.

21 I am twisting, just a little, the signification of what he says, to the extent that it signifies, in Nathan's context, that the dream is "realized" by way of the interpretations it receives. It is true that this metaphor indicates that the dreamer must head off on a quest for this interpretation, and that my twist is therefore only limited to (deliberately) erasing its interpretative dimension in favor of intensifying its ambulatory one.

22 Pons, *Le spectre et le voyant*, 161, 165.

23 Vilmos Keszeg, "Mort traditionnelle et mort accidentelle en Roumanie," in Bonnet-Carbonell, *Malmorts, revenants et vampires*, 49–72.

24 This plan not only made people leave everything, raze their houses, and go to live in apartment blocks, but it also created many victims, people not able to survive such a violent upheaval.

25 Chantal Deltenre, *La maison de l'âme* (Brussels: Maelström ReEvolution, 2010), 117.

26 Christophe Pons, "L'humanité élargie par le bas? La question des mort-nés," in *Faut-il faire son deuil?*, ed. Pascal Dreyer (Paris: Autrement, 2009), 253.

27 On this topic, what prompted me to extend the regime of confidence and its contamination "bit by bit" is the work of Jean-Marie Lemaire and his "concertation clinics": www.concertation.net.

28 Ekaterina Anastassova, "Entre le rêve et le rite: L'art d'apprendre à être mort," in Bonnet-Carbonell, *Malemorts, revenants, et vampires en Europe*, 193–201.

29 I have treated the question of organ donation with a xenograft approach in the chapter titled "X for Xenografts: Can one live with the heart of a pig?" in my book *What Would Animals Say If We Asked the Right Questions?* This problem gives rise to another that I will leave to one side in the present text: the relation to dead animals, and more specifically, those that die to nourish our bodies. Over and above the questions of what is right or not, and which may never close with a satisfying answer (as Donna Haraway reminds us in *When Species Meet*), is the problem of thinking that these kinds of dead receive none of the considerations that I am trying to describe here.

30 I am indebted to Thibault De Meyer, who pointed out to me Nowenstein's book (Farnham, UK: Ashgate, 2010). His aid has been essential in most of my research. One could also read, for a very different perspective because American law requires, unlike the French, explicit consent: Cantor Norman, *After We Die: The Life and Times of the Human Cadaver* (Washington, D.C.: Georgetown University Press, 2010). In the special issue called "Les morts utiles" of the journal *Terrain* (2014) can be found an article by Vivien García and Milena Maglio showing that the very status of the dead has changed under the influence of these practices: "Redéfinir la mort: Entre nécessités pratiques et discours éthiques." A part of this chapter also appears in the Introduction to this same special issue.

31 David Le Breton, "Prélèvement d'organe," in *Le Dictionnaire de la mort*, ed. Philippe di Folco (Paris: Larousse, 2010), 843.

32 Maylis de Kerangal's much discussed novel takes up, in a very concrete way, all the procedures that allow health professionals to negotiate families' agreement. Maylis de Kerangal, *The Heart*, trans. J. Moore (New York: Farrar, Straus and Giroux, 2016).

33 Joan Didion, *The Year of Magical Thinking* (New York: Alfred A. Knopf, 2005).

34 On this point, see Lydia Flem, *Comment j'ai vidé la maison de mes parents* (Paris: Seuil, 2004).

35 The philosopher Jean-Luc Nancy gives an account of this experience, and he asserts that it caused him to rethink the very question of his identity. Note that becoming "other" for Jean-Luc Nancy did not manifest the same waning of the feeling of being "other" that other testimonies have reported. Jean-Luc Nancy, *L'intrus* (Paris: Galilée, 2000).

36 This suspicion is reinforced, as Nowenstein shows, by the law of presumption of consent and by the fact that adhering to it is left to the discretion of the health professionals.

37 Laura Perichon, "Pistes ethnopsychologiques pour une lecture des relations que les endeuillés entretiennent aujourd'hui avec un proche décédé" (thesis, Free University of Brussels, June 2013). Perichon adds, following this meeting, "I must say that Rose-Marie's testimony had a big impact on me. In fact, when she said she wanted to make contact with the receivers, and, if they have children, that she would be a grandmother, I had to think hard. I realized that my whole conception of personhood, and of the (dis)continuity between life and death, between the body and the 'spirit,' between one body and another, was what Rose-Marie was questioning with what she was doing."

38 Elsewhere, the gift that allows the dead to be present at several places at once (and even more when several organs are distributed) gives these organs a status approaching that of the relic. Not just the fact of their ubiquity—they live in several places in little pieces—but also if one takes into account their vitalizing and metamorphic powers—they transform those they touch. They are even more similar if one considers the doubts and uncertainties that relics and grafted organs give rise to about their origins. Thibault De Meyer sent me a passage from a book by Umberto Eco. He tells me there is a chapter devoted to the place of origin and location of the tombs of the Magi. There are hundreds of tombs that say they have some remains, a finger, or a cartilage, of one of the three kings. Eco closes his chapter by saying, "Pilgrims in life, the three kings became postmortem vagabonds,

creating their multiple cenotaphs." Umberto Eco, *Histoire des lieux de légende* (Paris: Flammarion, 2013).

39 Michèle Fellous, "Soi-même et un autre: L'identité paradoxale du greffé," *Cité,* no. 21 (2005).

40 The last lines of a poem a mother wrote for her dead child. They can be found in Klass, "A New Model of Grief from the English-Speaking World."

6. UNCERTAIN THOUGHTS

1 Alexa Hagerty, "Réenchanter la mort: Les funérailles à domicile en Amérique du Nord," *Terrain,* no. 62 (2014): 120–37.

2 [The French is *meurt en détail.*—Trans]. On this point, one could compare this conception of death to that of Leibniz, who saw it as a swelling, an involution, an infolding.

3 Alexa Hagerty, in "Toward an Anthropological Theory of Mind," ed. Tanya Luhrmann, *Suomen Anthropology: Journal of the Finnish Anthropological Society* 4, no. 36 (2011): 59–60.

4 Tanya Luhrmann, *When God Talks Back* (New York: Knopf, 2012), 320.

5 Luhrmann shows, incidentally, that this theory of mind that is thought to be universally human, is not always as such. Joel Robbins, for example, reports that the Urapmin in Papua New Guinea say that they cannot know what someone has in their heart, or their thoughts, feelings or intentions, even if they express them. Too many things pass from the heart to the mouth for any words to be worthy of trust. The source of what is said is not in the intentions of the person speaking. If you ask an Urapmin what she means by what she just said, she will reply that she doesn't know; the signification is now in the court of the person to whom the words were said. We learn elsewhere another aspect of this theory of mind: a huge number of cultures do not establish the same distinction as ours as far as the events that deserve to be called causes go, and those that should be called intentions. An illness, for example, for which we look for a material cause, can be from another perspective, a sign that an offended being is claiming reparations. Joel Robbins, in Luhrmann, "Toward an Anthropological Theory of Mind."

6 The story goes that the night before the first trip her young musician son took, for a project called "The Troglodyte Project," Félicianne was

feeling really nervous about his leaving. Her son was calm, playing the piano in the living room. Then the cat came into the room and deposited a dead wren [*troglodyte*] at the feet of the musician. Was it by chance? "Why did Patch suddenly bring back a wren? Our cat had never brought back a wren, and she had never brought her prey back into that room where the piano was. Why now, when Ian was leaving the next day to Angers for this project? What was she sensing? What did she want to tell us?"

7 In an unpublished draft manuscript titled "Notes on grief and belief/ aporia" that she was kind enough to send me.

8 "Intériorités/sensations/consciences: Sociologie des expérimenta- tions somatiques du Contact Improvisation et du Body Mind Cen- tering" (thesis, Université Pierre-Mendès France, Grenoble, 2014). David Abram, *The Spell of the Sensuous: Perception and Language in a More-Than-Human World* (New York: Vintage, 1996).

9 Duperey, *Je vous écris*, 224.

10 Laura Perichon, "Pistes ethnopsychologiques pour une lecture des relations que les endeuillés entretiennent aujourd'hui avec un proche décédé."

11 Email, April 30, 2014.

12 Nanou, "Le mort est un invisible, pas un absent," in Dreyer, *Faut-il faire son deuil?*, 125.

13 Commenting on a first version of this inquiry during a meeting of GECO in Brussels in February 2012.

14 It seems to me this is one of the readings that might be given of Wi- told Gombrowicz's *Cosmos,* trans. Danuta Borchardt (New Haven, Conn.: Yale University Press, 2005) that radicalizes the experience of signification: if everything is a sign, the world is lost in an excess of connections.

15 In another register, Luhrmann notes that thanks to transcultural stud- ies, Americans are much less tolerant than people of other cultures of the fact of hearing voices, and that these voices are much more brutal. She says the fact of thinking there is a wall between one's mind and the world makes experiences of breaches of this wall all the more uncomfortable. But I would like to draw attention to the fact that she indicates, in passing, that the voices behave in an uncivilized fashion, and I think this should be related to what she discovered during an earlier study of homeless women in Chicago: she says she was begin-

ning to think that if people who hear voices that upset them "develop a respectful relationship with these voices, the torments diminish"; *When God Talks Back*, 20. I would add that this is something one has to learn to cultivate. I have learned a lot of very concrete things on this topic, and about respectful ways of addressing oneself to such beings, from Dingdingdong, the institute for the coproduction of knowledge about Huntington's disease; https://dingdingdong.org.

7. PUTTING OUR TRUST IN SPIRITS

I owe the title of this chapter to Marcos Mateos, email, March 26, 2014.

1 Christophe Pons, "Réseaux de vivants, solidarités de morts," *Terrain*, no. 38 (2002), 127–40.

2 Participation in séances is the last of the "instructions" I followed. It was a piece of advice suggested to me by one of my friends, Ginette Marchant, who had herself attended ten years earlier. I was a little reticent, imagining the worst extravagances, which explains why I didn't act on this instruction until much later. But it was an injunction, and so I ended up going along, encouraged by the fact that she offered to come with me. There we found (and I hope I can do justice to it) considerable humor, generosity, and intelligence. Ginette Marchant continued to go to the center long after I ended my visits on any regular basis. She was, in any case, an excellent intermediary, arranging a meeting with Michèle, the very talented clairvoyant, for a fascinating lunch.

3 Jay Winter, *Entre deuil et mémoire: La Grande Guerre dans l'histoire culturelle de l'Europe* (Paris: Armand Colin, 2008), 137.

4 Hagerty, in Luhrmann, "Toward an Anthropological Theory of Mind," 60. Emphasis added.

5 For example, Michèle would say to us, "Here we have the right to speak of that," with the implication that *outside,* things are not so clear.

6 Many mediums further explore these breaches via a third path. Their lives are often characterized by trials and tribulations to do with death: either they have been through sickness or have lost one or several children. Michèle is no exception to what seems to be typical: she herself was the victim of several accidents, some of which should have been mortal, and she has had several illnesses. Her son was born with part of his arm missing, prefigured in a dream. I'll come back to this.

7 In the choice of this term, I am going along with Tobie Nathan, who suggests giving up on the too loaded "possession" in favor of this term for someone acting a presence, "presentification." This term is all the better in that we are in a formation that is following rules of sociality and conviviality, and in which the clairvoyant "presents" the deceased to her recipient, the deceased in turn presenting himself by becoming present. See Tobie Nathan, *Philtre d'amour* (Paris: Odile Jacob, 2013), 43n1.

8 Bergé, *La voix des esprits,* 51. I would like to emphasize here, since I am talking about it, the immense interest in the investigation carried out by Bergé. Not only did the ethnologist strive to "speak well" of those whom she reports on, but she herself tried, as she says, to "engage on the other side of the mirror," in particular by devoting herself to automatic writing and by submitting the results of this apprenticeship to her interlocutors, the mediums, her "teachers," and by subordinating her research to opening up the space of a "why not?" This, in brief, as she says, comes back to getting out of a position of exteriority, which cannot really pretend to know its object well, by "giving something of oneself" (180–81).

9 Bergé, *La voix des esprits,* 30.

10 Bergé, *La voix des esprits,* 53.

11 The idea of starting by exploring conflicts, among consulting families, that are "practicable" before focusing on those that could prove to be "impractical" is due to Jean-Marie Lemaire, who implements it in therapeutic settings. See www.concertation.net and in particular consultative sheet no. 1 and consultative letter no. 7.

12 See on this subject, and which inspires me in this analysis, Claire Averty, "Le deuil et le rapport aux morts: Dimension thérapeutique de séances spirites" (master's thesis, Free University of Brussels, June 2013).

13 Jean-Bertrand Pontalis, *Traversée des ombres* (Paris: Folio, 2005), 46.

14 Tanya Luhrmann, "Making God Real and Making God Good: Some Mechanisms through Which Prayer May Contribute to Healing," *Transcultural Psychiatry* 50, no. 5 (2013), 707–25. Thanks to Thibault De Meyer for pointing out this important article to me. Furthermore, one might think this theory of social support appears as a distant avatar of the attack Freud would have directed against American religious therapy, an attack William James speaks of in very critical terms in

a letter to his friend Théodore Flournoy in September 1909. On this point see Drumm, "Des rapports aux morts: Freud ou James?"

15 Not only did James passionately study so-called metaphysical experiences and take an interest in the powers of mediums, but he also wrote about ghost limbs, on the same theme of exploring the limits of our experiences, our consciousness, and our perceptions of the body.

8. PROTECTING VOICES

1 Gillian Bennett, *Alas, Poor Ghosts: Traditions of Belief in Story and Discourse* (Logan: Utah State University Press, 1999), 275.

2 I would like to compare the form of inquiry that Bennett is leading to the fascinating work that sociologist Nicolas Marquis has carried out in a completely different field. He decided to study personal development textbooks in a very different way from that of sociologists, who usually show contempt, mistrust, and disdain for them. He uses the tools of reception theory and rearranges them from a pragmatic perspective, and with great tact: How do readers find an account of themselves in these books? What do they make them do? How do they help them or transform them? He shows the similarity between the relationships established between the readers of these works and what Donald Winnicott calls transitional objects (such as the baby comforter). Marquis quotes the latter: "There is an agreement between us and the baby that we will never ask the question: 'Did you think of this yourself, or was it presented to you from the outside?' The important thing is that no one is expecting a decision on this point. The question itself does not have to be formulated." Marquis remarks, and this is the comparison I want to draw here, that when he invites the readers of these works to explain, during an interview, the process by which they give the text the authorization to affect them and the way in which this text directly touches them—when the investigator puts the reader on notice to justify his feeling of effectiveness of the book—the very fact of asking the question prompts the latter to explain the experience in such a way as to destroy it, instead of preserving the coexistence of the two possibilities—was this message in the book or was it I who (over)interpreted, who created it from scratch? "It is therefore by successive points of contact, reading between the lines of the readers' words, that cooperation must be described"; Nicolas

Marquis, *Du bien-être au marché du malaise: La société du développement personnel* (Paris: Presses Universaires de France, 2014), 128.

3 Gillian Bennett works not only with her father in Manchester but also with her daughter Kate Mary Bennett who was a psychologist at Leicester University at the time. Vanessa's testimony comes out of an article they wrote together: Gillian Bennett and Kate Mary Bennett, "The Presence of the Dead," *Mortality* 5, no. 2 (2000), 149.

4 Interview in Perichon, "Pistes ethnopsychologiques."

5 I have for a long time called this process equivocation, first to mark the equivocation constantly in action, then to refer to the concept of translation as elaborated by the anthropologist Eduardo Vivieros de Castro, and finally, the third reason, aligning myself with the etymology (*vocare*), to indicate the fact that there were two voices and one does not know which one is speaking. I abandoned this term in particular because it polarized the statements too much. I give a more precise account of the reasons that led me to abandon it in Vinciane Despret, "Les morts font de nous des fabricateurs de récits," in *Gestes spéculatifs*, ed. Didier Debaise and Isabelle Stengers (Paris: Les Presses du Réel, 2015). For equivocation as a double translation process, see Vivieros de Castro, "Perspectival Anthropology and the Method of Controlled Equivocation," *Tipiti: Journal of the Society for the Anthropology of Lowland South America* 2, no. 1 (2004), 3–22.

6 Bennett, *Alas, Poor Ghosts*, 260.

7 David Hufford, "Beings without Bodies: An Experience-Centered Theory of the Beliefs in Spirits," in *Out of the Ordinary*, ed. Barbara Walker (Logan: Utah University State Press, 1995), 11–45.

8 This interview came from the thesis by Margaux Doutrelepont, "Le rapport aux morts chez les personnes maghrébines à Bruxelles."

9 Jean-Marie Schaeffer, *Pourquoi la fiction?* (Paris: Seuil, 1999).

10 Antoine Hennion has made us particularly aware of how to identify what, among amateurs (understood as those who know and cultivate particular modes of feeling, which makes me want to compare them to Luc Petton as an artist), testifies to a very special way of being attached to the world. Hennion's pragmatic approach is all the more fruitful and instructive (in the sense that I understand this term) in that he allows himself to be traveresed / transformed by these attachments, which he invites us to consider as attesting to a "reflexive, corporeal, framed, collective, equipped activity, producing in the same movement the

skills of an amateur and the repertoire of the objects to which he is attached." Antoine Hennion, "Pour une pragmatique du goût," 2005, www.ensmp.fr. [See also Antoine Hennion, "Pragmatics of Taste," in *The Blackwell Companion to the Sociology of Culture,* ed. Mark Jacobs and Nancy Hanrahan (Oxford: Blackwell, 2004), 131–44.—Trans.]

11 Daniel Bensaïd, *Walter Benjamin, sentinelle messianique: À la gauche du possible* (Paris: Les Prairies Ordinaires, 2010), 40.

12 Roland Barthes, *The Pleasure of the Text* (New York: Hill and Wang, 1975), 9–10. This is where I see the contrast between dealing with *death,* and *the dead* in another way. Death, as analyzed by the sociologist Geoffrey Gorer, has become "pornographic" insofar as it can no longer be seen or evoked, thus replacing sexuality, which can be spoken of and seen. The dead, in the limited context in which they can come into their own and generate narratives, would be erotic. It remains to be seen, however, whether the theory of mourning and the prescribed obligation undergo "a mourning process" that today seems prevalent everywhere, are not, as Dominique Memmi's reading suggests to me, a new standard obliging people, in the same way as we observed with regard to sexuality, to offer power a control over intimacy. Geoffrey Gorer, *Ni pleurs ni couronnes* (précédé de *Pornographie de la mort*) (Paris: EPEL, 1995); Memmi, *La revanche de la chair.*

13 For acts as "workshops of being," see William James, *Pragmatism: A New Name for Some Old Ways of Thinking* (Cambridge, Mass.: Harvard University Press, 1975), 138. Thanks to the philosopher Stephan Galetic for showing me this passage.

posthumanities

Cary Wolfe, Series Editor

Vinciane Despret is professor of philosophy at University of Liège and professor of ethology and sociology at Free University of Brussels. Her books include *Women Who Make a Fuss* (with Isabelle Stengers), *What Would Animals Say If We Asked the Right Questions?* and *The Dance of the Arabian Babbler: Birth of an Ethological Theory,* all published in translation by the University of Minnesota Press.

Stephen Muecke is professor of creative writing in the College of Humanities, Arts, and Social Sciences at Flinders University, South Australia, and Fellow of the Australian Academy of the Humanities. He is coeditor of *Latour and the Humanities* and coauthor of *The Children's Country: Creation of a Goolarabooloo Future in North-West Australia.*